FRAGRANCE AFTER RAIN

FRAGRANCE AFTER RAIN

JAIYA JOHN

Soul Water Rising

CAMARILLO, CALIFORNIA

Printed in the United States of America

Soul Water Rising
Camarillo, California
soulwater.org

Library of Congress Control Number: 2021916469
ISBN 978-0-9987802-6-9

First Soul Water Rising Edition, Softcover: 2021

Inspiration / personal growth and healing / spiritual growth

Editors: Jacqueline V. Carter
                                      Kent W. Mortensen

Cover and Interior Design: Jaiya John
Cover photo: Jaiya John

During one of my childhoods, the distant rain curtains would sweep toward me over the New Mexican mesas, sweetening the air with their pregnancy. I could feel sky crying. I wanted to cry with it. Here, now, with you, I offer those sacred sky-tears.

– Mshkiki Odeh Inini
(Jaiya John)

AUTHOR'S FIRST BREATH

I HAVE PRAYED LONG over these words. Watered them with all my heart. I hope you are present with them. Not in the way a student is present in class. In the way a mother is present with her newborn. These words want the milk of your Love.

I was moved to scatter the seeds that are these words freely within the book, to create a wildflower meadow you may enjoy wherever you lay yourself within it for a moment and breathe beautifully. These petite stories and mystic whispers are entirely liberated from chapters and sections, freely roaming, drifting on spirit breeze as they wish. Each word-bouquet is growing and gathered according to the sunlight, shade, soil, and water of Love's orchestral conducting.

I like to think that if you open this book, turn to a page, and your eyes arrive to a brief orchard of words, and your heart tastes the fruit and meets its craving, that those particular words are what you need in the moment. I like to think this is a book of bright clouds in the sky of your life. Bringing you beauty, meaning, the downy reflection of sunlight, life-replenishing rain, and a sweet fragrance thereafter. My heart hopes you can walk, dance, sing, and repose yourself through this aromatic pasture, and feel a due peace that is both medicine and music for your soul.

HOPE IS AN HEIRLOOM passed down the generations of souls in morning (mourning). A treasure shared between those on the simultaneous shores of pain and paradise. Hope whispers a secret of how living things remain alive. Hope sings. Sings in notes tuned to the range of human despair and defiance. Hope is a rope you swing over the canyon chasm of fear, swinging above the murky sediment of doubt settled at the bottom of the polluted river of pessimism. When you release your tears to flow down your cheeks, those tears are hope messengers on their way to your heart. They have something fresh and fragrant to deliver.

Hope is a resurrected Light. Behold as it reanimates what has surrendered to thoughts of doom. It is that impossible breeze through the wide window that puts to sleep the candle flame, then returns to bring the burning back to life. Hope is a reunion with the surreal peace ever inside your divine nature. It brings you to that palace, opens the door, hosts your visit, serves you nourishment, and grants you a soft bed and fresh sheets for supernatural rest. Hope is a home. Hope is a dawn, a dusk, a turning. Hope lives in your yearning.

Hope speaks in the dialect of Promise. The stories it tells are of legends and mystical happenings that reason says could not have happened. Hope is not reasonable. Not seasonable. Hope is an everlasting atmosphere. Hope is untamed, incorrigible, feral, and free. Hope cannot be discouraged. It is a titanic waterfall that drowns your discouragement, sweeps you to the ocean where breeds

9

of hopeful things migrate in the deep decadence of being.

Hope bleeds. Its sanguine outflow expels from you the accumulated toxins from your lifetime. Hope expunges the long record of your personal harms. Hope is not a judge or jury but a trail guide pointing you toward the place of your reckoning. Hope places your duty in your hands and sets you off to shape that clay.

Hope purifies your persona. Weaves peace through your dense jungle of worries. Hope is a medicine wheel. It offers you the four directions, four teachers, four elements, and the ancestral assignment: *Care for each other no matter what.* Hope is a dreamcatcher. It snares your skepticism, burns it in the blinding brightness of Grace. Hope delivers the sacred dreams that hold your valleys of tall grass, clear water, and circles of ceremony among living things.

Hope rises. It is lighter than your lightest ideas. Just when you believe Hope has died, Hope rises again. Even in the crevasses of your pain and loneliness, Hope rises. In your private self-disgust and disbelief in this life, Hope lives there, too. Lifting as a mist, spreading its gospel until that scripture becomes the entire sky. Hope burns your sacred plants. Hope is the plant, the flame, the burning, the smoke, the fragrance, the spirit, the clearing. Hope is a cathedral glistening through the stained glass, vibrating in the bellows, reaching for the arches, polishing the wood for prayer.

Hope is in the silence you suffer and savor. Hope laces your laughter with a friend. Hope musters your courage to touch what in this world you feel dearly needs to change. Hope scatters fertile seeds in its wind. Hope's long fingers plant in the soil. Hope is a water feeding the sprout. Hope is the sunlight to greet what breaks through from the crust of ground. Hope is what rises and fattens and blooms into fruit. Hope is in your biting, your eating, your robust renewal.

Hope is your awakening when you pause long enough, are hit hard enough, are awed deeply enough, lose enough, are emptied enough, rendered and shuddered to the bone. Hope opens your eyes. Dilates your heart. Suffuses your breath and body with the oxygen of determination.

Hope is the gift Grace offers you today. A flower that will not wilt. All that is Love is Loving you in this present breath. All that you are feeling is medicine for our great healing. And though you may feel your ordered life has fallen, be comforted in this ascendant Truth: Hope is a Miracle. Already risen. In you.

WHEN SUNRISE SWEEPS her hopeful robes over your heart, you feel the flush of new life. A prayer that sings of birth. Of sweet deaths of release from your yesterday suffering. Stay in this river, friend. Move through day marrying peace over and over. The prophet in you wants to shout from the mountaintop, of the glory you have seen. Open your timid voice. Dilate your music. Give us the lion who makes clear the passion in its roar. Give us the songbird chorus of clouds. Spell beauty with each heartbeat. Translate the code of Grace for those wandering in ugliness. Break bread with silence. Pour wine for the wind. Wind your way out of the forest of conformity. Sprint out into the clearing where the bleeding poor have gathered. Laugh to the brink of drowning in tears. Let them drink freely from your spring. Share yourself with Day like this. Voyage all the way out of you. Return soaking to your soul. Taste union and explode. Firework your feelings like a child. Cherish their brilliance, weeping gratitude like a waterfall in Love with this holy life.

JASMINE TEA. Bubble baths. Essential oils. Candlelight. Prayer. Meditation. Walks in the wilderness. Cups of silence. Laughter to tears. Liberated crying. Sacred dancing. Soulful singing. Gardening. Making Love. Making music. Poetry. Passion. Baking. Breathing. Exercise. Sleeping. Resting. Dreaming. Creating. Cleaning. Journaling. Learning. Teaching. Guiding. Listening. Healing. Mobilizing. Solitude. Quietude. Surrender. Remember. Release. Sage. Cedar. Sweetgrass. Sacred tobacco. Sweat lodge. Sunbath. Swim. Explore. Discover. Cherish. Affirm. Care. Compassion. Love. Ecstasy. Tremble. Gasp. Glow. Glory. Grace. Ground. Tearfulness. Dilation. Epiphany. Nirvana. Euphoria. Solace. Solitude. Sunrise. Sunset. Dawn. Daring. Mess. Mystery. Majesty. Mystic. Drumming. Humming. Moaning. Melting. Awe. Aura. Pause. Flow. Touch. Cradle. Nurse. Suckle. Wean. Wander. Wonder. Womb. Soaking. Floating. Flying. Flame. Seeing. Pulsing. Kissing. Thrilling. Night. Now. Nectar. Summit. Sigh. Mist. Break. Birth. Bold. Beautiful. Subtle. Privacy. Intimacy. Treasure. Chocolate. Water. Spice. Succulence. Serenity. More Jasmine tea. Whatever it takes. Stay in your ceremonies. Stay rooted in wellness. Hold your peace.

FEEL YOUR DEEP DESIRE for peace. Close your eyes. Let the world go. Let your inner world come back awake in you. Hand on your heart. Hum in your chest. Medicine. Hum your Love. For all things. Let the warm vibration run through you, a stream dissolving your adhesions. Dissolve yourself. Let your ideas release into sky. Let your bones cry. Your blood mist. Your muscles surrender. Open the stable doors. Allow your anxiety to escape and return to the wild.

Wilderness. You are a wilderness living in a cage. Step out. Look around. Shake off your slavery ways. Deep breath now. Act like freedom. Brave the unfamiliar air of your new way of being. Your life of permission. Grant yourself things. Joy. Healing. Mercy. Grace. Grind the spices of compassion. Mix with heartbreak tears and drink. Feel your molecules rearrange. You are becoming your original spirit. If it feels naked and vulnerable, it is because your old false walls that never protected you are crumbling. True safety feels like bare skin in the breeze of an unobstructed sky. True safety is determined only by your soul. Not how you are treated on earth. But how you live in your sacred invisible world.

Float on your back on the water. Gaze blue sky until you find yourself as blue sky gazing back at you. You were never here in the way you thought you were. You were always outside, looking in the window, inheriting stories from others. Now be inside this happening. Weave new stories from the yarn of your heightened instinct. Wear those medicine blankets now as you sleep and in your daily labor. And choose new air to feed your thoughts. Breathe something beautiful. Let it be fertile soil for the fertile seeds and sprouts of how you think and see and feel this life that cannot be corralled. Shed your tired arrangement of cells. Choose this new expression of you that resembles a miracle with its mouth open to Creation, ready to receive more miracles.

SOMETIMES, THE BEST WAY to get your life in order is to go wild and never be civilized again.

She wakes feeling wild. Walks down to the river. Plunges. Beneath the surface, she cries joy. Water washes away her painful stories. With them goes the pain. She fills with morning's subtle sermon, which is all the verses of Peace. Her body dissolves in the river. Now she is river, floating upon herself. Staring at pastel blue sky, hawks draft over, printing a calligraphy of grace on her vision.

Moon gave birth last night to a new litter of stars. She feels them now in her womb, dancing. She caresses her belly, feels a celestial Love bloom and soak her cells. Willows on the riverbank whisper in the wind. A powder yellow butterfly lands on her shoulder. She is its silent island in the stream. Waving her arms back and forth, water gently sloshing her skin, she feels an old rage get up in her chest and go walking. Away from her.

Today, she will make no plans. Perform no expectations. She feels so good she wonders if this is a dream. Her body flushes with pleasure. Heart rate slows like last raindrops from the roof long after the rain. Her clothes for this whole day shall be water, wind, and sun. She cries a pouring gratitude. She is undone.

IN THE DIVINE MOMENT when you were conceived, this one thing was true: You were intrinsically as beautiful and as worthy as any living thing. This has never changed. This will never change. Please proceed to Love and embrace yourself accordingly. *Peace-ify* your soul.

What if, dear soul, you lived your life as though you are entirely, absolutely, overwhelmingly good enough. In every way. What would your heart feel like. How would your pain river out from you. How would you treat yourself. And how awesome would be your aura of contentment and security, your persona of Freedom and legacy left of a soul who seeks no approval, inward or outward, but radiates as a heavenly nova in the universe. These are not questions. They are answers. Through devoted daily affirming practice, you can peace-ify your reality and be medicine for the world.

SILENCE CAN HEAL what constant noise has inflamed. Much of this noise is hidden within others, not expressed on their tongues. You feel it nonetheless. A violent tide against your delicate coastal flowers. If you are tired and your nerves are spent, consider absence as the presence you need. Consider more time in sacred silence.

BELOVED SOUL. When others live like volcanoes, you do not have to join their endless eruptions. Living in the passion of action and reaction, we suffer the abandoning of our peace. We can root ourselves in the divine constant, the placid lake that does not tremble when the sky shakes or spills its water. Practice allowing others their volcanic lives without joining them. You can be like the old tree. Unmoved and yet wonderfully engaged in life.

FOR THIS WORLD AHEAD we don't need more gurus. We need more translators of soul. The soul of the world is stirring. We are shedding old skins of oppression that constrict us collectively and personally. Catching the scent of freedom, like the fragrance of air just before rain. What is the soul of the world saying to you, dear one? What is your soul saying? Each of us can deepen our listening to these whispers, wails, and roars. They are always in us and all around us. They impart to us the path, how to walk it, and the meaning of release and birth.

Have you heard the soul of a sand grain? It can sound like the majesty of a mountain. And what appears broken can sing a most glorious song. Look not at the surface of a thing and judge it. Listen not to the shell of someone's speaking and miss the seed within. Quiet your soul. Settle at its center. Now you are a mirror to a world that beholds itself through your clarity. Translate the pain. The purpose. The yearning. The beauty. Tell us. Why does everything now tremble? How is grace polishing our looking glass? And what, oh what, is this overwhelming sunrise for?

BREAK BREAD. Break habit. Especially if it is bad bread. Break the status quo if the quo is a sickened status. Break your heart if it will let compassion run through you again. Break from the norm if the norm is a killer. Break the spell if the spell is not Love. Break out of bondage. Break into grace and share it with everyone wandering the streets. Break rank. Break deadly order. Break cosmetic beauty to reveal true splendor. Break up with fear. Break down the propaganda of power. Break-fast. Feast on soul and spirit again.

TAKE OFF THE REST of your fear-woven clothes, tender one. We need your naked truth. We have enough conformists in costumes. Only your true soul can help us heal. Once you set it loose, it may go wild and do things that astound you. Like bringing you a peace you cannot imagine. And pouring a beauty into the world that makes even hardened hearts swell and cry.

WHEN WE OFFER OTHERS a name for their suffering, a language and vocabulary for their experience, we endow them with the kinship, compass, keys, map, and nutrition for their own voyage out of cages and through the territory of healing. Share your words of kindred experience. It is a Love offering that yields life. Feeling like you need affirmation and assurance? Offer the same to another. Use your words. See how the energetic draft of your unique, caring expression creates an invitation from your soul to others to join you in relating common experience. Soon enough, the response arrives and you see the truth: You are not so alone. And your struggle was not so impossible. All you needed was the words.

LET US SPEAK OF GRIEF. One moment, in the ocean. Next moment, under it. One day, not on a calendar, the shore. Let us soft walk this season on earth, kindred ones. That when we reach the other side we may look back from the clearing into the dense forest and see the glory of purpose waving at us and saying *Now you see what all this was for.*

FRAGRANCE AFTER RAIN . JAIYA JOHN

WE SPEAK OF ALONENESS as a disease. Maybe the truer disease is our fear of being alone. Maybe the best companion we can be emerges as we lose our desperation for companionship. Togetherness thrives in openness and inner peace. Freedom.

HAVE YOU TASTED SILENCE? It needs no seasoning. Silence is the seasoning. In a world of continuous noise, both audible and energetic, silence can be a potent medicine and add soulful flavor to our life. It can heal mind, mood, nervous system, body, emotions, and relations. Silence is a meadow where our spirit roams and grazes on peace and inspiration. Even brief moments of silence can awaken clarity in our life and clear the window through which we see and understand our journey. A divine music is always at play in this world, inviting us to dance to its restorative nature. This music is silence. You are the dancer to whom it desires to whisper its most beautiful secrets.

THOUGHTS ARE LANDING PLACES for your feelings. Gentle thoughts make for soft feelings, like pillow and mattress cradle your body. May your thoughts be plush and kind. Invest in a new mental mattress, dear soul. It can reinvigorate your life. You are so worthy of peace that you were given an unlimited range of thoughts to practice and sow. No need to stay bent over the same tired rows, plucking the same tainted thoughts that pain and burden you. You can shift over to the brighter acres, where wonder and grace sprout organically and wave at you their invitation. Your soul is beauty beyond measure. It is a butterfly looking for a soft, sweet place to land. May you fill your mind with your favorite flowers. May you water them. May they grow.

ALL WORDS AND WHISPERS in Creation speak the same unchanging truth: *You are worthy of a beautiful life.* The essence of this beauty is sacredness. Sacredness in you and in all things. If you exist in such a way that you increase the beauty-glow in the lives of other living things, you symbiotically manifest beauty in your life. And what is the composition of true beauty? Love. Love is the confounding mineral and molecule binding together all that is divine. Love is the soil, water, sun, and air of your earthly garden. You cannot escape this truth. You cannot take an avoidant way around your pain and woundedness. Love is the only way. It courses straight through your suffering and parts the daunting water. Fear in you says you are not worthy of such paradise. Truth says *Follow me. I know the way.* You are worthy. This worthiness, dear soul, is the way.

EXHAUSTING LANGUAGE: *What am I accomplishing today?*

Revitalizing language: *How beautifully am I breathing today?*

Beautiful breathing can be cultivated, like a garden. Or an art form. It is an art form. The form of being present and released. Sculpt your peace by shifting from a task-oriented life to a centered, oxygen-infused life that enriches and optimizes your tasking. Each beautiful breath is a whole system cleanse. A divine download. A deposit in your life wellness account. Deep massage for your soul. May your breathing be as glorious as you are.

GOOD NEWS. Your thoughts are not your soul. Your pain is not your soul. Your soul is free. Your entire worldly experience swims around inside you. It is not you. You are the divine sky all things pass through. If in your daily life you can practice remembering your *skyfulness*, you can develop a freeing relationship with your thoughts and feelings. One in which you remain the central *soular* power of innate peace. In this way, you can feel yourself determining your life rather than being determined by your life. What feels heavy in your life, dear soul? Maybe you can plant seeds of lightness in that soil. How? By remembering your soul is free. We heal by remembering, which is a Loving act of letting go of our delusions. And opening to the scintillating persona of our infinity.

LET'S MAKE A DEAL. I will Love you. You will Love me. In the safety of that divine chrysalis, we will imagine each other only in beautiful ways. This will be our earthly medicine. And we will grow wings and live fluent in the sky of bliss.

ANYONE CAN HURT ANYONE. Lovers are the true sacred warriors of the world. Sweetgrass on the prairie sends up its prayer for us all: With ancestral memory as our truth fire, may we be brave enough to Love. May we be braver still and make a shimmering new world in that holy land.

YOUR TOMORROW IS THE CHILD of your today and the grandchild of your yesterday. It might be time for a family meeting. Harmonize your generations. Talk with your people (days). Make it good. Live beautifully now, as prenatal care for the future you are birthing. Most folks accessorize. Be one to *ancestorize*. Even a single self-healing act now begets healthier generations of days in your life. In all lives. Ponder your people (the days of your life). Season your pondering with peace.

IMAGINE IF YOU CELEBRATED and Loved yourself all day, every day. How much pain would be healed. How much bliss would grow in you. Nothing is stopping you, dear one. Party hard in the house of your soul. For some souls, the house party never ends. Dance. Sing. Laugh. Lose your bindings. This worldly thing can be crazy. Be crazier. Be your own champion. Plant praise. Harvest peace.

WHEN IT COMES TO LOVING yourself, what you may feel is a rain shower is only a light mist compared to the monsoon you deserve. Never be afraid to flood the valley of your soul. Never, sweet being, be ashamed to swim naked in the healing waters of your own affection. Your soul wants you naked and soaked in your inner romance. Not just now and then. With every heartbeat. Breathe deeply. Open your heart. Proclaim the poetry of your passion. Take the plunge.

I LOVE YOU. Doesn't matter if I don't know you. You don't have to qualify for my Love. That's the lesson. Bless you and Good Night.

Humans need more practice Loving and receiving Love. Maybe if the world wasn't so hardened, we wouldn't be so bruised or bruising. Be brave enough to soften your heart. Celebrate the softened souls. No more toxic celebration of hardness. It hurts. Role model being something a baby can cuddle against. Cause you're still just a big baby looking to cuddle. Don't even front. Also, tears are medicine. Let them flow so they can do their sacred work. Okay, that's all. As you were. Unless you were hardened. In that case: *As you weren't.*

DANCE IS THE BODY'S JOY and the soul's delight. The most wonderful form of dance is when you adore yourself. Love is ecstatic motion rivering through your soul. Bust out your freedom moves. Anytime. Any place. For no obvious reason. Send affection and joy through your molecules. Jubilate your hurt away. I don't know if jubilate is a word. If it was not before, it is now. I'm verbally dancing.

YOUR SOUL WILL NEVER COMPLAIN about you taking a big, beautiful breath. Not even when life is heavy. Especially then. Honor your divine design. Breathe.

When you blow wind through a wind instrument, it makes music, medicine, and wonder. You, dear soul, are a wind instrument. Breathe. Give your being continuous breeze. Then behold the music it makes. It is heavy now on earth because humans are remembering Freedom, and Fear is terrified of that. When faced with such energy, sing your sacred song of soul. Stay in your ceremonies. Especially in the storm. Stay in your music.

GATHER TOGETHER IN A CIRCLE. Invite your tears to gush. Collect them in jars of story. Pour them into a gourd of memory. Drink each other's water. Soothe your souls in moonlight. Return often, for freedom causes fear to rage, and this newborn world needs healers. Propose to Love.

I SEE YOU. I FEEL YOU. I LOVE YOU. I grant you safety on my soul lands. I breathe with you. I remember your ancestors and bow. I weigh your sacredness over your imperfection. I court peace with you before quarrel. I silence my opinions so I can listen to your truth, let it land on my heart and breed generations of healing. I worth your pain over my comfort. I kneel with you in the cold earth and plant warm seeds that carry all your sacred names.

This is how we coexist sacredly. And how we are to be safe human beings. Patient practice, for surely we stumble, fall. The dirt, though, is our renewal. It holds a grace that makes all things new. It is a mystic mother for what rises: the tender sprouts of our humbling. And in that condition gestates a sensitivity of the soul.

MAY ALL THAT IS BEAUTIFUL weep your truest names. May you gather that tear-water in your palms, stare bravely into your reflection, and see the face of your soul and its infinite parade of dreams. May you surrender to the staggering truth of it all and crumble into your new being, which is your oldest being, your ancient ceremony of soul.

LEARN IN A THOUSAND LANGUAGES to say *I Love you* to your soul. Your soul knows every language that was, is, and ever will be. It is a romantic and desires that you speak beautifully to it. Sit with it at cafés. Take it out to dinner. Cook for it at home. Walk with it by the stream. And if you really want your soul to sigh and cry and die of delight and be born again brilliant and aural, sing to it. Sing *I Love you* in all the languages that it knows.

REPAIR THE HARM. Feed the garden. Saturate the soil. Fill the well. Re-rain the sky. Moon the sun. Sun your soul. Salivate freedom.

MAKE LOVE YOUR CEREMONY. Stay in your ceremony.

WHAT ARE YOUR MEDICINES? Bring them to the fire. We are in a healing time. The age of conquest is over. The age of freedom has begun. Go get the drum.

SHE WAS DETERMINED to grow acquainted with her true soul. It would be her gift to herself. To all living things.

As we discover our purest, unconditioned, unpolluted nature and calling, we transform from hurtfulness to medicine. For ourselves. For all our relations. May you know your true self, a reflection of your collective self. May it be a patient, passionate Love affair.

HERE IS TRAUMA: You are harmed inside a cave. You peer out of the cave into a sunlight you cannot believe. You are afraid of the sunlight even as you want it. You extend your hand out from the darkness into a sunray. You are terrified. The sunlight feels good. Yet it feels so foreign that you tell yourself it feels bad. You retract your hand. You go on like this, timidly extending parts of yourself out into the light, being conflicted at how it feels, not trusting that the light is safe, that it won't hurt you, retreating back into the cave.

In the cave, you suffer. It is the source of your harm, of your continuing harm. But the longer you exist inside the cave, the more you grow a cruel kind of comfort. A familiarity. You weave false stories about how you belong there, in the cave and its harm. Stories about how the light will surely harm you. Eventually. Stories about how unworthy you are of the light. These stories contour and condition your nervous system. Even thinking of being in the light, your body reacts. A sick feeling courses through you. You shake and tremble and grow nauseous. All from thinking about the endless expanse of daylight outside the cave, and your ability to stay alive in that light.

In time, you gather your courage and leave the cave. Your whole body steps into the light. It feels amazing, but so new and unfamiliar that you cannot possibly trust this feeling, or its source. Slowly, with your whole body tensed and curled in, your breathing shallow and quick, your eyes dilated and your heart pounding, you go wandering. You encounter incredible beauty that your mind labels as ugliness, as danger. You encounter streams that flow into waterfalls, waterfalls that pour into lagoons, lagoons that flow into rivers, rivers that bloom into wide lakes. You come upon massive trees with boundless canopies. And wildflowers everywhere.

Birds sing beautifully but you interpret the sensation as harm. You interpret the trees as potential harm, and the waters that run and the grass that grows and the animals that approach you with Loving hearts and the breeze that cools you and the sun that feeds your skin and the earth beneath your feet that holds you and all of the sky and all of Creation, you translate all of this as potential harm, potential enemy, potential pain, unbearable pain like you experienced in the cave.

Your stories now lead you to yearn for the illusory safety of the cave, of the strange comfort of predictable harm, a harm whose face and form you at least can recognize, a harm you know deeply. You weave stories that reason why you need to return to the cave. Now. Immediately. And never leave the cave again. You weave stories that resign you to a fate of spending the rest of your lifetime in the cave, with the pain you know. *The pain you know.* This is trauma. Which, though daunting, is only a cloud in the bright sky of your life, of your being, of your medicine story to come.

HERE IS THE THING about human suffering. We take its infinity and break it into categories that do not exist. So that we may be conditional in our compassion. So we may withhold or let flow our Love and action according to how we have been trained. When the humans who suffer are those we have been trained to spite, especially trained by caste power, we trap their suffering in glass jars of justification that preserve its fermentation.

When those humans with whom we affiliate suffer, especially those elevated by caste power, we open the floodgates of our Love and shatter all the glass jars and wail at the world: *Pay attention to the suffering of these premium humans, and proclaim and perform how much you care about the suffering of these premium humans or we shall shame you.*

Here is the thing about human suffering. It is not human at all. It is the pain of Life without category or condition. It is a fateful fire burning through the entire forest of this universe. Human suffering is not at all convenient for our trained prejudices. It makes mockery of our favor and disfavor. And while we withhold our compassion and dehumanize suffering humans to rationalize our compassion withholding, human suffering spreads among and within us.

Here is the thing about human suffering. It will destroy you no matter where you hide if you do not destroy all the glass jars of its fermentation. If you do not prioritize collective freedom over your personal prejudice. If you do not demolish the dam obstructing your heart. If you do not place in a fire pit and burn all the narratives of who and who does not deserve to freely exist, then burn the ashes that remain, then burn your memory of these flagrant stories...

If you do not end these stories, it will be the end of you and those you Love and all your premium humans. You will not exist. Because human suffering is not a game you play that can be placed back in its box when you are done for the moment arguing why you do not care about *less than premium humans*. No. It is not a game of opinion. It is a rampaging wildfire and you are the deadfall already in its ravenous path. It is you who are soon to be ash. The only hope for you and your Loved ones and your *premium humans* is to shatter all your glass jars and die. Die out of your life of glass jars and be born into the truly living world where living things care most of all for the faintest suffering and purest freedom of living things. Unconditionally.

SHE WANTED PEACE. So she forgot all she was taught, and remembered herself.

I pray for you. That your peace be not a 17-year-cycle cicada waiting deep down in the soil of your soul for a brief fling with flying, mating, reproducing. That your peace be an entire inner sky of liberated butterflies painting your whole life with the colors of their useful wings. That today you forget just a few of the reasons you are unhappy, and stumble over strange foreign things on your path. And when you bend down to pick them up, you discover these foreigners to be reasons for your joy. I pray you put them in your pocket. Or swallow them on the spot.

I pray you place the pain of your grief in your palm, then blow on it like a dandelion seed. And that, even if just for a moment, this seed takes flight away from you. I pray you can remember what lightness feels like in your chest. And that you speak to your tears softly, saying *It is okay, my sweet emotion. You can pour out now freely. I won't punish you at all.*

I pray today you will pray by breathing with your every molecule. That maybe you imitate the birds in song. They gather near you because they are curious why you are songless. They Love you and want to share with you their verse. I pray you take their gift and become music. That your new sound drowns out the old life that haunts you, and an audience gathers to enjoy your lush melody. I pray that this audience stays long within you. Breeding fertile its enthusiastic, grateful peace.

ONE MOMENT YOU ARE LAUGHING, the next crying. They say you are emotional. I say you are all the way alive and bathing in life's sensitive river, which is a water made of emotion. Life is an emotion. Feel it.

I see you in the lagoon. Early sun watching you, smiling. You are dressed only in a gown of water. Water at your waist, glistening on your skin, adorning your eyelashes, beaded and dripping from your hair. Now you are in the waterfall, feeling everything you have ever felt, at once, baptized in the truth of it.

The gushing shower over you is receiving your most naked confession. All the feelings you never admitted, not to you or anyone, are pouring out of your heart. You are in shock that your heart could have held so much. It did not. All those feelings were stored in your bones, *Querida*. Stored in your marrow and corpuscle. Held captive in your cells and neurons. Sheaths of emotion clenched your organs like a fatigued fascia that wanted only to be released.

This soul water rushing over and through you now is your perfect masseuse. It touches your every plot of pain and bruise of memory. It hurts. But it hurts so good. One moment you are laughing, the next, you are the waterfall, releasing its entire volume of sacred music in tears. Your saltwater ocean spills into the freshwater lagoon, which rises and swallows your breasts in its purity. Birds in the canopy have arrived and are in awe. Squirrels are bowing on the bark. Bowing at the sacredness of your nakedness. Of your release.

Willowy white clouds above have paused their drift, watching. Soil and stone are watching. Everything stares at you in wonder. One moment you are a nearly bursting gourd holding all the feeling of your lifetime. Now you are a beautiful gushing that cannot stop crying *Glory, Glory* at every fertile grain of moment and meaning you are graced to live.

SILENCE WORKS LIKE THIS: Sometimes, you need to hear nothing. So you can hear everything.

Out here in the desert, she could feel her soul. The impossible silence was the thing. She could not escape herself, the way the silence looked at her. The way it spoke. Nothing stood between its compassionless voice and gaze, and her lifetime of denials. It obliterated her defenses. All her habitual stories betrayed her, went running out across the burning dirt and bleached shocks of shrub. She knew she needed this demanding treatment. So she came here often. Sometimes walking in a daze. Sometimes lying on a large, flat boulder, letting the sky give her a subtle kind of facial treatment. Now and then, she felt fear, so alone. Mostly, she caved into the solitude and crumbled. This kind of dying felt good once she let it take her. Breeze loitered around her like an animal looking for her to feed it. It fed her instead. Out here, in the desert, she could feel her soul.

IT CAN BE FRIGHTENING to encounter one's gift. And so we run away. We approach again, trepid. We toe the water, we run away. We breathe deeply and try again, this time submerging up to the ankle. This is water we have not touched before. It is foreign and fathomless. We tell ourselves *I cannot do this, this is too big for me, I am not ready, I need to retreat and go get more ready, I need more qualifications, this is for other people, special people, I cannot see myself in this water.*

On and on we go like this, flirting with the water, our gift, talking ourselves out of it, running away. Some of us eventually find the will and the reason to jump in the water, submerge our whole being in our gift. So many more of us spend our lifetime in this dance of approach and retreat, often countless times in every moment. Our fear dutifully shepherds us all the way to our last days, we having never made peace with our gifts.

Our whole life we carry a yearning, a weight of wanting, ever knowing, for all along, in the very center of our essential being lies the water, our giftedness, and we can see it. We can feel it. Yet we will not let it be. Our gift does not taunt us. We taunt ourselves, in every single moment. Unremittingly.

ALL MY LIFE I HAVE SEARCHED for a more perfect music than silence, a more perfect companionship than solitude, a more perfect protector of my heart than Love. I have found none. I open these blessings that open me.

PLEASE REST, QUERIDA. *Descanse*. Repeatedly exhale your guilt and toxic tasking stories, and feed your whole life with the root medicine of rest. If you want your life to bloom and bear fruit, please, please feed it rest. I Love you. Not love as a possessive, needful, frightened spirit. Actual sacred Love. Like when a child sees a butterfly trapped in a jar and sets it free.

FOR BREAKFAST, she sat on a blanket in the meadow and had guava, mango, and papaya. For lunch, she swam in the lake and had almonds, plantains, coconut juice, yams, and berries. For dinner, she lay on a soft quilt, ate dates, figs, potato stew, and avocados, drank lemon water, and made Love. She was well fed this day. No shame or guilt. No task anxiety or nervous planning. Just a sweet moment of indulgence that would become a wealth in her memory.

To manifest a beautiful life, it helps to envision a beautiful life, to witness a beautiful life, to dare our first timid steps into a beautiful life. Even against the insidious tyranny of oppressive labor, precious, pleasurable daily rebellions are possible and numerous across the world. Do not deny yourself the pleasure of dreaming, dear soul. For to become a butterfly in flight, first you must birth a faith in the divine glory of your wings.

WHAT BRILLIANCE ASLEEP inside the soul of one who grants the will of the herd ultimate authority. Be you willing to wander and graze the neglected grass, you will find your soul-stone shimmering up from the riverbed, and sunlight's qualities will bloom in you.

MAYBE. JUST MAYBE. Your restlessness is your soul saying *Here I am. Take me. I'm yours.*

We cannot run from the sun inside us, dear one. Be true. Be you. Life is a journey of accepting yourself. As you are. Regardless. Taste your organic sweetness. Devour your honeycomb. Surrender to you, and know peace.

MAY I WHISPER SOMETHING to you? There is more beauty in the world than you know. Keep opening your heart. Only an open heart has eyes for beauty.

The river of healing runs most lushly through an open heart. I have been gathering peace all my life. First, the

33

hills were steep where it grew. Sharp thickets everywhere. Then, over time, the land gentled. Pure, clean water appeared more often. Peace was more abundant there. I learned to track the sign and scent of it. And that its territory is within me.

I have gathered peace all my life. Please, lean this way. I will send some peace over to you. I hope you will use it to soften your soul and open your heart. Especially in this moment. Especially in the ones to come.

TONIGHT, YOU WILL tell yourself only Love stories. You have to feed sweet dreams. Sing your soul to sleep this way:

I LOVE YOU.
I LOVE YOU.
I LOVE YOU.
I LOVE YOU.
I LOVE YOU.
I LOVE YOU.
I LOVE YOU.
I LOVE YOU.

TODAY. Today you open the flower that is your heart and take in the ethereal sunlight that is Love. Today, you bloom. Today, like all days, can be springtime in your heart. Love is in you and all around you, as the ether and nectar of life itself. Things do not have to be going well for you to taste Love's bouquet. All you need do is lean like a willow into the breeze of any beautiful thing and breathe its fragrance. All you need do is arrive like a bee to a blossom and let yourself be blessed by the awesome aura and persistent pollen of Love. Which is life, the unexplainable vibrancy and Grace of gratefulness.

WHO IS AMONG US? For we do not know. And yet we treat our relations with the same desecration to which we treat ourselves. We cast as mundane what is divine. Pollute what is pure. Make unsafe so many sanctuaries. We spit on the sacred and do horrors to the holy. Who is among us? For we do not know.

Forever are we shocked and silenced when a scorned and unadorned human is revealed to be the Word. When who we looked down upon and disbelieved and devalued is shorn of rags, cleansed of dirt, and stands splendid as the Impossible Light. Who is among us? For we do not know.

In this fallen world, ever open your heart and surrender to your knees in Love. Glory is not gone. It is in the ground and growing. Grace is not defeated. It is on the mount, in the sea, and risen. In every moment, It is risen. Who is among us? For we do not know. Do not wait for evidence from the tomb. Believe. Behold. Die and be risen. Die and rise among us.

THE CHALLENGE is not to become sacred, but to recognize that you have always been sacred. So that you might live sacredly. A sacred life is rooted in the soil of a sacred identity. Believe you are innately sacred, and not the desecrated thing a desecrated humanity has deeply conditioned you to believe. As you nurture and cultivate your sacred identity, your sacred ways emerge, at first tender sprouts, in time a majestic forest of choices, energy, attitude, behavior, affect, memories, ceremonies, relationships, and offerings.

You are a sacred soul on earth. You do not have to qualify to treat yourself or be treated sacredly. You are kin to earth, sky, water, and fire. You need not conspire. Onward in your sacred ways, you bastion of Love, woven of suffering and solace. Make this life beautiful. Or rather, be a vessel for the beauty of this life.

IF YOU ARE NEITHER SAFE nor honored, it is not Love. Do the patient labor of being safe and honored within. You will find your way home. Your soul will sing again. Homecoming. Reunion. The way out is to journey in. Lean also on your faithful trees. They will hold you up in the wind. Safety is in your DNA. Somewhere in your brilliance, you know the way. You are waiting for you. I send you Love.

WE WON'T BE HERE LONG. Let's be gentle. When we feel those brushes with our mortality, fragility, and the brevity of life, it has a way of sweeping us into a compassionate heart-pose with what we hold precious. May we extend our gentleness to all living things. Grace lives there, too.

HERE IS MY LOVE LETTER FOR YOU, dear wanderer. You deserve to be alive while you are still alive. Be all the way here in your life. Activate your whole soul. Breach fear. Surface. Heaven is in the spray and mist. Feel things. Feel them all the way. Testify. Open your mouth. Risk censure so you can breathe. Elope with your passions. Marry freedom. Tremble. Gush tears. Sea turtle yourself across the sands of captivity. Awe-stun the predators. Reach ecstasy's ocean. Become its holy water. Evaporate. Gather as rainclouds. Monsoon. Drink your own pouring. Be soul water for this arid, aching land. A divine and magical thing is happening. Your life. Come and join it in the precious brevity of its season. It is blooming for you. Bloom back.

BEAUTIFUL SOUL. Let who you were and who you will be... hold *who you are now* close and long like a Lover. Gravity is not the only thing holding you to this fickle earth. You need affection from the collection of your many *yous*. Be your greatest Lover.

BEYOND ALL THE PAINFUL STORIES you tell yourself lives this truth: Your soul is beautiful. You cannot change this, no matter your self-loathing. You might as well surrender. Bathe in your beauty, dear one. Your soul water is the perfect temperature. For you and only you. Soak yourself silly.

IF YOU HAVE LIVED YOUR WHOLE LIFE in a cave, it can be hard to believe in sunlight, or in your nature and capacity in sunlight. For a slave, this sunlight is freedom. Nurture yourself Lovingly as you come to believe in your life beyond the cave.

FRIEND, DO NOT ENTER this dance floor if you do not want to do this sacred dance. Everyone here is losing their minds so they can remember their souls. And the only music playing is Love.

SPEND THE REST OF YOUR LIFE learning the true song of your soul. Its mystic music will set you free. Why download other people's tracks when you can soak in the sound-bath of your greatest hits? Your soul song can heal you. It is the mating call that will bring you home. Learn its melody. Peace will sprout and bloom in you. Its joy-fruit soon bursting forth everywhere. Stillness. Beautiful Breathing. Catch the sacred tune.

LET US BE CREATOR'S GRACE in this world. Our Love will be the sacred maize fattening on the autumn stalks. We will be in the children's laughter like bright silk lifting in air. When we gather for ceremony in our regalia and the smoke dances, so will we with night-long endurance. Let us be the Grace in the river that makes it shimmer. And the soft compassion calming our anger and aggression. And when we are given endless opportunity to judge and condemn each other, our Grace will not let us wear that false and infected security blanket. Instead we will cry mercy with all our might, knowing in our breast and bone how dearly we need mercy's shower to Grace us, too. To Grace us, too.

EARLY MORNING DEW sits lightly upon its many Lovers. No leaf or blade of grass or patch of dirt complains of having dew's clear jewels on its face. You can practice letting your morning thoughts sit this lightly on your heart. And if you fill your day with sufficient Love-light, like evaporating dew, your morning thoughts will burn away. Sky will gladly take them. What collects in your mind at night need not burden your next day. Thoughts and feelings can come and go, condense and evaporate, if you let them. You are the gatekeeper, dear flower. Your heart-blossom can remain free and light if you stay in dewy relation with the sky that is your life.

THERE IS AN OPENING in your soul. If you move through it, you will find another opening. If you move through that, you will find another opening. And another and another. On and on. All of these openings are you. You are not a thing. You are an opening. To all things. All things are an opening. To you. Keep opening.

You are an opening, Querida. This means your natural state is to be open, dilated, for Love, life, feelings, memories, visions, music, medicines, and energy to come through. For *you* to flow through you. You do not protect yourself by closing, but by opening. You are a kind of sky. Your wellness is in your *skyfulness*, in your expansiveness and breeze (breathing). As you gather bunches of wild peace like wild berries or wildflowers, you become a doorway to serenity, an open window through which all things sacred flow and fly and leave and enter. You are the wind and the wind chime. The bird and the birdsong. Beauty and its flower, fragrance, and flourishing. Open, BeLoved. Into your *you-ness*. Soothe suffering with your boundless being. Let pain be awed by your endless territory of healing. Let your spirit gasp and sigh and channel the sacred ceremonies of your soul.

YOUR BOUNDARY NEED NOT ALWAYS BE an angry electric fence that shocks those who touch it. It can be a consistent light around you that announces: *I will be treated sacredly.*

Exude your mantra, you precious soul where peace resides: *I will be treated sacredly.* This is how you reclaim your sovereignty. In the light that goes before you. As you grow secure in your self-determined safety, you see that you don't always have to bark, roar, snap, or growl. These techniques may feel necessary in the moment, but often they feel so by habit and fear, not by present circumstance. And they damage you with inflammation and toxic energy that spill into the world, harming it and you. It is okay to try a gentler way first, for you more so than for others. Practice treating yourself with self-Loving boundaries. These habits become energy that then becomes your aura. You may be amazed by how people notice and defer to your example. Teach on, dear soul. Teach us sacredness.

JUST AS IDENTITY can be a ladder out of your suffering and fear, it can be a tar pit that drowns you if you clench it desperately. Hold your identity like a light cloud in your heart. Let it morph as you discover your soul endlessly. Let it graze on Love and roam freely the wilderness of the world. Fall in Love with your identity but do not marry it. Elope with your soul. Stay supple. Have no rigid ideas of who you are, so who you are may dine on breeze in the morning and feast on moon tonight.

SHE OPENED HER HEART to her entire life and Loved it all, even the pain. To her surprise, a new kind of joy flooded her empty spaces. Gardens bloomed there. She became a butterfly and drank the nectar of her own existence. She birthed bliss.

May you open your heart and soul to Creation, dear spirit, and be filled with Love's eternal medicine. May its potency overwhelm your suffering, leave you gasping and breathless in ecstasy. For surely, if you open, Love will make Love with you. You will become a kind of ever replenishing river in the dying desert. A pure crystal stream in the thick forest of agony. Touching everything with Mercy. Leaving a raw, unfiltered weeping in your wake.

If you dare be undone, dear flower, your caress will undo the tension in living things. Hard rocks will blush and bloom into the finest, softest beds and pillows of down. Pain will open its purse and gift you its patient gatherings. Ugliness will die before your divine mirror and repent. Frogs will dance on the shells of turtles. Jasmine will perfume your path.

Intoxicated, you will sing a mystic song of hope. Only the touched will hear its luminous notes. Their hearing will suffice, for, entranced, they will dance the sacred Sun dance in the tall grass of your summer until their bodies break and their generations of hurt are released. The veil of this world will fall. Every soul will admit its fear and dissolve in your river. All of this is in you, you nubile treasure. When you open. All the way. And make all things new.

WATER YOUR LOVE. Sun your compassion. Shade your hate. Cradle your fear. Feed your dreams. Spread your kindness. Light your passion. Sing your soul.

Gardening tips for a beautiful life. For a beautiful world. May you heal your sweet soul and arrive further than ever into Love's mystic garden. Its fragrance will intoxicate you and your deepest desire will be to pour out your Love, that all living things may drink from that sacred water and be nourished on their own journey to the divine ocean of healing. May we mend this world. One beautiful, heart-opening breath and courageous reckoning at a time. These words are my Love for you.

IF YOU COULD SEE, you delightful spirit, the good things to come, your heaviness would evaporate, and you would cry thankfulness for this stretch of your wondrous road.

EACH DAY, SHE FORGAVE herself fully and started over. It was her secret recipe for a light heart. And peace.

And you will flower again, and wear the joy in your heart as jewelry of your aura. And music will sing itself through the streams of your blood. And your molecules will dance delirious again. And Hope will receive your Love letter and come back to you. And there will be passion and purpose growing wild on the hillsides of your days. And you will pick them like the freshest berries and devour them with the glee of a child. The juices will color the windows of your perception. Your energy will be art. Your dreams will grow softer. Your memories gentler. Your prayers like the lightest clouds of gratitude. You will live through this ponderous *Now* and arrive at a priceless land the angels call *Beautiful*. And there will be crystal rivers, and reason growing like tall feather grass. And there will be peace, dear soul. There will be peace enough, forever.

IF YOU WANT PEACE, dear one, prepare a garden in your heart. Peace is a butterfly looking for a place to land.

I keep a place for you in the garden of my heart. Beside a pond where sun gazes its reflection. Clouds of jasmine fragrance drift. Bees browse the abundant flowering. Hummingbirds drink blossom nectar. Dance drunk and true. Butterflies paint mystic murals in the air. If you need more peace than this, there is a fountain with clear water from a mountain spring. Put your lips to the flowing, and recognize your true Lover, Grace, kissing you sweetly in return.

SOME ACHING FEELS surreal. Mystic. Like a portal to a world where tears don't fall. They flower.

We are all in pain. Relate to the world from this premise and you may find yourself soften. Including your pain. So much wonder and Grace in being alive. Still, to endure this world, we, like all living things, inherit the generational pain of existing. Presume this tenderness in others. It explains so many imperfections and causes for your grievance. Why inflame with anger, judgment, and malice when you can touch the beautiful, bruised sweetgrass braids of another's journey and realize you are touching a kindred braid in the weaving of your own life?

Unwell souls teach you to be a tyrant on earth with no tolerance and passionate prejudice. Love is always teaching in another classroom: *Compassion*. Sign up for Love's ephemeral course. Attend even on your weary days. Especially then. Take notes. Better yet. Take off your armor, part your curtains of fear, and embody the lessons. We need you to soften, so you may tell us gentler stories of how to treat you when we find you, and how we can, despite the colonizing seduction of oppressive spirit, manage to soften together.

We are not painless. None of us. What grace we manage is a triumph. Let the rains of mercy soak you. In your next breath be more like cotton than you were before. Be a lush meadow of sighs even the most harmed of us can lie upon and feel safe enough to soften, too.

CLASSIFY YOUR JOY AS SACRED. Grow a prized garden of ceremonies around its heart. Plant seeds of small graces.

Slow sing the stalks. Indulge peaceful moments. Let them ravish you. Birth bliss. Never wean it. Of your tender moments, fashion a temple. Pray there in sweet tears. Release your moss of pain. Bathe long in your soul waters. Sigh holiness.

EACH MOMENT IS AN ORCHARD. Meaning is its fruit. Eat your joy like a child in summer heaven.

YOU MAY STUMBLE OFTEN as you heal and grow. Take comfort. Falling is a kind of rising. The downdraft that births the updraft. The weather system prior to peace.

You will fall. There will be dirt and stone and blood and fear and also a tourniquet of faith and tonic of mercy. And somehow through the doubt you will rise and hear your true name in the wind. You will grow wings and reach for it. And you will fly. Oh, how you will fly.

The soft landings, safe spaces, and ecstatic flights you dream of are dreaming of you, Querida. You are the fantasy. Do you see? Oppression is a nightmare. You are the waking. Your pain and joy are pointing the way. People will judge you as though they know you. Go about knowing you, and you ascend beyond judgment. People will seek to bottle you up. Shatter their bottles with your freedom cry. Colonizers will claim you. Claim your great unlearning. These words are not a riddle. They are the romance. You are the candlelight at the table where healing sits and feasts.

ARE THERE HUMMINGBIRDS and hope in the stories you tell yourself about yourself, dear soul? Are there butterflies laughing? If not, maybe they are not your stories. Maybe you have not yet found your stories. They wait for you.

Funny thing about our stories. Many of them are not our stories. We inherited them from family, friends, strangers, society, and past generations. Some stories live in our bodies and brains as energy, moods, fear, anxiety, stress, trauma, inclinations, sensitivities, and disease. They are a talkative bunch, gossiping with each other day and night about you, about the world, about things that are not true.

Here's another thing about stories. They are tribal. They like to hang out with each other along kinship lines. And they may not like to move out of you, but they Love to move in. So find ceremonies and rituals, daily practices that help you identify and release stories that are not native to your soul. And daily practices that invite your true, native stories to move in. These native stories are your true people. They Love you. They carry Love. They come from Love's oral history. You can know them by the way they make you feel: not artificially good, but organically nourished. They sing you to sleep like an angel. Wake you with a sunrise of hope. They affirm your divine nature. Regardless of how the world treats you. Your native stories see you. Reflect you. Hold faith in you.

Remember your sacred names. Here is to your unweaving and releasing of the stories that are not yours. And to your weaving of your intrinsic stories. They are your medicine. Your freedom. May you find and nourish your circle of relations who can weave this sacred sweetgrass with you. May you deepen and nourish your

46

personal weaving out in the solitude of sunsets and silence, and in the rich lands of your inner reflections. Your innate, ancestral stories are a sanctuary. A home. You are safe there. In the essential rivers of your soul.

EVEN YOUR MOST PRIVATE kindness creates a public ripple. Kindness matters. It fertilizes all that is beautiful. Kindness is radical revolution in a hostile world. Tender is the medicine way. May you walk good on the path and touch inward and outward with a paintbrush of compassion. You are a muralist. Suffering is the canvas. Kindness is your paint.

YOU DEAR, SWEET, unanticipated singularity. Can you look deeply into what hurts and call it holy? Then you shall be a sanctuary unto your soul.

HER NERVOUS SYSTEM had been through so much. She decided to spend the rest of her life calming the inflammation. Thoughts, feelings, memories, behavior, relations. She soothed it all with deep, Loving breaths and gentle practices. The softer she became with herself, the softer she became with the world, which in many ways became softer with her. She birthed a new generational cycle: Unrepentant Peace.

Can you land on this harsh earth like a downy feather and not lose your soft essence and offering? Then please float the down-currents and be among us, and we will call you *sacred medicine*, and drape you in the sky as a kind of moon. And coyotes will cloister in the wash of your glow. And they will howl a deep pitch. And mystic things will stir. And the land will breach-birth a timeless time. Umbilical blood will feed this newborn era. And your oldest dreams will, like eggs, crack and open and yield fresh life, wet and winged and already tasting flight.

IF YOU DARE TO WALK the dark alley of your despair with a persistence until dawn, you will meet a stranger. This stranger will pour you cups of tea and offer you a warm blanket by a friendly fire. This stranger will sit with you and tell stories and laugh heartily at your own. Your tears will gather themselves in heaps and billows and pour from you with a power you cannot contain.

The spilling will not be polite or pretty. No room for performance lives here in this moment of reckoning. No, your pain will rampage forth from you like a desert flashflood in a summer monsoon. Your tears will be an absolute ocean of eruption. Your crying will be heard in the stars. Your body will collapse. Finally. Your theater of composure will dissolve like molecules in the wind.

You may think of being embarrassed or humiliated, but at this point you will not care. For the stranger will be holding you, rubbing your back, and supporting you in reassuring tones. Now you will feel something wet and cleansing birth and grow and become *you* from the inside out. You will feel as though you have become a blissful lake. Later you will call this lake *Triumphant Peace*.

Then, as dawn's candlelight first touches the sky above the alley and begins to spread down into your ink of fear, the stranger who has comforted you through this terrifying communion will begin to fade from your view. You will search the alley, now brighter by the moment, looking for the one who sat with you, who sewed up your serrations with kindness. The one who whispered to you *Hope* in a language you had not known. You will search and you will search until the epiphany blooms in you bold and rich with color: The stranger was your true soul. The stranger has not disappeared, but has reanimated in your being that has always been its home.

Your soul and you will sit for a while and cry together, sweetly, as doves applaud from rooftops. Then, the two of you, now manifest as your divine and inseparable oneness, will walk out from the alley that is now sun splashed and new. And new. Will be you.

AT THIS VERY MOMENT, you are ravenous with desire. Your mind tells you that you desire a certain thing, person, outcome. But can you take hold of the wet root of your desire with your bare hands and follow it down to where the root begins? For it is likely that what you believe you desire is but a story obscuring what your soul truly wants. And what it wants it already is. The appetite and the fulfillment exist as one radiance in the divinity of who we are. The soul is an eternal aching for itself. This, dear one, is what you hunger for.

LOOK AT YOU. Each day, your soul is becoming a more beautiful art.

I want to behold you grow old and more beautiful in my eyes. I do not yearn for you to be young and unformed like early clover. I desire the fullness of you. The seeping of your soul into corners and crevasses of your elusive being. The bloom of serenity in your chest. Sunrises in your skin. Sunsets in your eyes. Broad winged wonder that takes your breath. Small, multitudinous laughter at things the younger *you* was too serious for.

The vast glory of you learning gentleness with yourself. The sweetness of your vulnerability. You chasing your short-term memory through the day. Evolution of how you carry your pain, from tight chest bundles into a rosemary mist diffuse within.

The beauty you choose. How you polish your letting go. Grief songs you learn. Shame you shed. New debuts of honesty. Final curtains of performing to please. Original aspects you reclaim, from before the harm. Your late romances with joy and lightness. Spring cleaning you do in your soul in winter. Practicing trust and safety in your private courtyard of solitude. Your modest consideration of changing to light. The gaining nearness of that eternity river and the way it leaves its holy fragrance on your shores. You humming heaven here on earth. Learning new music at dusk. No longer capitalizing your fear. Flowers. All the flowers you become.

ALL OF YOUR PLANS and planning have led you to this place you could not have planned. And now you are crying. And there will be pain. Difficult places. If you avoid the difficulty, there will be pain. If you move through the difficulty, there will be pain. If there will be pain regardless, why not take the path through pain that brings you to something beautiful? Sometimes the sun will be too bright. Will you still give it thanks or will you search for caves? A land exists between planning and not planning. Nomads call this land *Freedom*. Ancient ones call this land *Peace*. No matter what you call it, it calls to you. Turn the soil there. Plant your life.

IT IS MORNING AGAIN. Sun is fresh. Your soul is hopeful. Dreams are rounded up in the kitchen. They want to tell you their sacred names. Pour your coffee. Sit. Spend a moment playing with your dream children. They miss your company. You will always have the business of your day. For now, be fresh. Sip tea. Flirt a while with peace.

WOMAN. You got taught since you were a girl to bury all your belongings. Now you cannot find them. You have been a good student. Now you bury your pain. Your suffering. The untidy truth of your motherhood. The wilderness of your womanhood. You bury your rampaging womb desire that burns through your bones, a glowing river aching for oceans of release. You bury your steam rising from that simmering surface. You bury your dreams with each breath. You bury your grievances. You won't say *Stop*. You won't say *You can't speak to me like that. Treat me like that.*

You won't up and move. The burial orders continue: *Be a good little girl. Bury how you feel about this arrangement of men. Of women trained by men. Bury your intelligence. Your way of seeing, of being, of moving, of weeping like living things have need to do. Bury your ancestral power. Bury you. Woman.*

But your soul has decided another life. No more burials. Now you pull your living artifacts from obsidian ground like pulling roots for village stew. You unearth bright things bandaged in black clinging soil that smells like womb. You disinter your unoppressed spirit. You bring it from the dark depths beneath stones and water tables. You breach your entire being up through the crust.

You must. Woman. Take this personally. Tribal-scarify yourself to freedom. Go forward an enchantress chanting all you have buried. Tell all your stories. In your way. To your circle. Stay wading in the dawn water. Unbury your primal pulses. Your ceremonial instincts. Cast dirt aside and walk on the surface of earth. Learn to be above ground and whole. Learn to be a sun-stalk bloomed and pollen-blushed and painting sky.

Breathe all the air. You weren't meant to inhale mud just to survive. Kill your burial teachings. Wrap yourself in softness, gentleness, firmness. Summon strength of trees. Woman. Eat freedom. Discover your true face unburied and beautifully blemished. Treat your voice like a kite. Stay in the sky. Make friends with clouds. *Lightness* is your sacred name. Call yourself all the words your soul uses to soothe itself. Siphon what makes you happy from what makes you holy and drink deeply for the rest of your days.

IF YOU FIND YOURSELF often annoyed, irritated, maybe others aren't always the cause. Maybe the pain in your soul keeps you chronically inflamed. A horse with a bur under its saddle will buck and throw any rider, no matter how faultless the rider. Until the bur is removed, the horse will remain in a state of irritation. What is the bur in your soul? Heal that, and you may find it takes far more to irritate you. So primed will you be to be at peace.

YOU CAN'T HEAL without the feel.

When we carry trauma, often the last thing we want to do is feel. We grow numb to try to survive. But in the end, feeling is the only way to healing. Organic feeling is our medicine. Our repair. Guided, nurtured feelings move through our tenderness as an ointment, soothing and restoring our soul tissue. A soul massage if you will.

We can't think our way to healing. What was harmed in us in the first place is a feeling thing. That feeling thing, our being, responds most deeply to emotion. The root tonic for hurt is not thought. It is Loving feelings. Gather your Loving guides and dare, drop by drop, to feel it all out of you in healthful ways.

To fee or not to feel. That is the question. The way we numb, suppress, deny, avoid, bottle our feelings, we are subtracting from our being so much of what we require for our healthy existence. We lobotomize our emotional self. If we lobotomized our thinking, our mental intelligence, we would be less able to manage this world. More vulnerable. We do the same by eliminating our relationship with feeling.

A hard river came into you. A soft river needs out. No matter how long your drought, your feelings want out. You can gradually grow into feeling safe and free while being a feeling thing. Just imagine how your soul would sing. It has been holding so many beautiful notes and lush lyrics that all flowing things know by heart.

IDENTIFY YOUR TRUE medicine. Hold it close. Drink its blessings often. Permit healing.

TRY NOT TO QUARREL with your intuition. It is trying mightily to help set you free.

TRIGGER WARNING:
I am going to tell you I Love you.

If it is hard to hear these words, the gift is that now you know the place in you that needs your healing work. Especially if you struggle hearing these words most of all from you. Love is not a reward for good behavior. Let go of that childhood fairytale. You are worthy of Love. Actual Love is safe. What isn't safe is living outside of actual Love. No more banishing yourself, beautiful soul. Go home. Acquaint yourself with being Loved. By you. Once you live in your Love, all Love expression will feel like your native song.

SHE PREPARES PLANTAIN, yam, fufu, mofongo, cassava cake, and sweet mint tea. Her ancestors will be joining her tonight in her dreams to discuss her path, their path, to freedom. They will be starving.

EVERYBODY IS SCARED. You aren't afflicted. You're alive.

When you step outside, you feel air on your face. This is freedom. When you are alive, you feel fear in your body. This, too, is freedom. The sensation of possibility. Yes, things could go wrong. But what if they go right? What then? Are you afraid? Congratulations. You are alive. Beautiful things are still possible. You are one of them.

SHE WOKE ONE DAY believing in her healing more than she believed in her suffering. Her soul rejoiced and flowered.

Belief is how you water your soul garden. Belief does not grow from a beautiful life. A beautiful life grows from belief.

WHEN YOU COME NEAR SOME SOULS, their energy is like paradise unfolding on your shores. You want what they have. But, dear one, they have been working in the soul garden for lifetimes. Where, dear one, is the dirt of your labor? This is not judgment, it is Love pointing the way. The paradise of peace is not gifted to us. It is a treasure we find deep down in the dirt of our healing labor.

DO NOT BE AFRAID to treat yourself sacredly.

If you have not always treated yourself so well, it can feel strange, uncomfortable, and even vulnerable to treat yourself sacredly. As though you don't deserve it. As though it will not and should not last. Especially if the people in your life do not treat themselves sacredly, or did not treat you sacredly as you were growing up. Breathe peace now, dear one. Even small, bashful steps will get you to a sacred life.

Sacredness is a habit. In a world that pollutes, cheapens, and desecrates the sacred, it is up to you to champion, celebrate, and role model living sacredly. Do not be afraid to believe that you are a sacred thing. Do not be afraid to call yourself sacred. See what miracles happen when a sacred thing exists as a sacred thing. You have so many *soulrises* left in your life. And you are ever worthy of beautiful things. What are your sacred ways? Naming them brings them to life.

MANY PEOPLE WEAR beautiful jewelry, yet do not feel worthy of a beautiful life. Jewelry can be a prompt to make you feel beautiful and worthy of beauty. Try wearing some on your soul.

REVIVE YOUR TRUE LANGUAGES. Restore your customs. Recover your land. Heal your relations. Host peace. Give ear to your ancestors. Weave new stories. Re-throne your native beauty. Distill medicine from your suffering. Build a fire. Welcome those who Love your flames. Ceremony the night. Make dream offerings. Soul-bless the day.

FREEDOM IS NOT a favor granted or received. It is the persona of life. Seek to be alive while you are alive.

IF YOU DARE to create something beautiful, you might just bless someone's tenderness. The art in your heart is not just for you. Nor does it want to be born so it can be judged, weighed, or categorized. Some soul somewhere is a receptor cell for the spark in you yearning to be created. Release your inspiration. Have faith that it is medicine. And that someone needs its special tonic. Grow used to sharing your medicine. Watch how it returns to you and gives birth to your own healing.

THIS WEIGHT IN HER CHEST, pooled like heavy water in the basin of her molecules, had been with her all her life. It felt to her like an overdue birth. One that threatened her life. It was the particular weight of being a woman. And of being Indigenous. As she reflected on her lifelong fatigue, the persistent awning shadowing her life, she yearned to break free from this scar tissue binding her to suffering. Something else rose in her as well. Rage. Rage at this imposition. Determined rage to claim her joy in her lifetime. Not in the lifetime of the generations after her. *Now.* She was passionately devoted to tasting joy on her own living tongue.

SUN IS A LOVER. Open, if you want its passion. Be sun-like if you want to be a better Lover. To all things that could use the purity of your passion.

YOU HAVE TWO PLACES of emergence within you. Two sources from which you speak energy into the world. One is an inner well composed of your uncared for pain. When you speak from this place, you bring your private torture out into the world. You spread your suffering and blanch life from living things.

The other place in you is a wellspring of vitality. This wellspring is filled with the consequence of your healing work. It is a place of emergence that bears sweetness, like honey from the ground of your being. Like manna from the heaven of your spirit. When you speak from this sweetened place, such fruit comes forth from your lips, valley after valley is seeded, and vast orchards grow in the hearts of souls. People feast from your fertile offerings. Generations are nourished and sustained. When you speak from your sweetened place, you are a grower of worlds.

Much of your life is a matter of which source you choose to speak from. For what you speak does return to you, exponentially. Remember, when you came here, although you carried two ancestral wells within you, your true soul hoped for a lifetime of drinking from the water of reprieve. The healed and healing water of peace and effervescent life.

THIS CHANGE you are considering. That terrifies you with what could go wrong. Have you considered what could go wrong if you don't change? What already is wrong because you have not changed? Have you weighed the worth of what could go right? Remember, your whole life has been change. You're still here.

HAVE YOU WORKED OUT your joy today? Make sure to get your reps in.

In a depressed, anxious world, you can train your brain for joy. Your brain is imminently teachable. A faithful student. It develops an appetite for the thoughts you feed it. Live each moment, from the pain to the passion, as though it is a miracle. Allow tears of awe to soften your soul. This is how you flood your brain with wonder and all the wonder chemicals that heal you. As your brain becomes wonder-full, joy moves in, takes up residence. Then joy takes over your brain. Joy is a gifted interior decorator. You're going to Love what it does with the place.

A GROUP OF POETS DYING OF THIRST in a boiling desert arrived at a pool of water. The poets cried gratitude. Then, they saw their reflections in the water and cried at how unpresentable they felt themselves to be.

The desert itself was confused. *Have I not offered you lifesaving water?* The desert asked. *Yes*, the poets answered. *But look at what your harsh conditions have done to our appearances*, they grieved. The desert's heart dropped. It could not believe dying souls would reject its offering to instead focus on its extracted toll. *I thought if I removed your source of vanity, you might more deeply appreciate my gift of water*, desert replied.

This conversation went on and on until night. The poets could no longer see the pool of water, even in the starlight. They had wandered too far. They were done. The next morning, crows picked at their pockets, pulling out poems on paper that they carried off to use for making their nests.

Sometimes, we grieve because we lose sight of our blessings and have fallen in Love with our captors: *complaint* and *lament*. Drink the water, dear soul. You have more poetry left to share.

YOU OPEN A WINDOW wanting fresh air. Fresh air enters wanting fresh soul. Maybe. Just maybe. You are more precious than you know. Reappraise your worth, dear soul. You have no idea how Creation wonders at you. Maybe much like the way you wonder at Creation. You are a bright thing coated in a lifetime of false ideas about yourself. Go down to the soul water. Time to wash your spirit clean.

ALL MY LIFE living in the palace of my body, thinking it to be the palace of my soul. A new sun gleams the horizon today. I see now what all along Creation has been whispering to me in Love notes of breeze and sky. I am a soul. Which is my palace. And Grace, the keeper of all that lives there. Including my body.

And when fear and pain visit my window, and I strain to hear Hope's music in the trees, I sing a supple song to myself that stirs peace inside my sanctuary:

I am ordained in this season of my life. Ordained in robes of change. Goodness has bestowed upon me a single red blossom in the meadow of my wellness, a tender flower that needs to be touched and healed. The rosary of my life moments comforts me on my chest and in my hands. I polish its brilliant beads by remembering I am Loved.

My whole life I have been feasting in the orchard of holy fortune. I am maiden to the River that knows me so well. Along those warm banks my Loved ones remain gathered, singing and crying and laughing with me. These are the days I tend the blossom in the meadow that needs my touch.

I am not hostage within a long shade of misfortune. I am free and frolicking in the bright sun of circumstance. Even my tenderness is a celebration. My weariness rests itself into a resurrection of my life's vitality. Where I am uncertain in my being, Spirit shines the way. Oh how I am remade in the womb of Providence. My soul is my palace. Eternity the countryside where my palace stands.

I breakfast on fresh peace in the morning. Take my midday cups of serenity. I am Loved. I am Loved. I am in the meadow, nurturing the needful blossom inside of me. All that I feel is a string of notes in the music of Sacredness. Beauty has come to talk with me. I am in this, this moment I have been given to bathe my soul in uncertainty.

Fate brings me close to the tall, wide window so I can breathe a blessed air and sunlight can touch me with its affection. I am new in this journey. I am new in this amber meadow. I am new with each pulse of change, with every ache adorning my existence. Love is not my distant observer. Love is with me, in the spirit of all I Love and who Love me.

Love is my sermon, my medicine, my giving rain. I am floating on an impossible sea of holiness, in waters that bear my weight. I am weightless. I am in this moment, already giving itself to the next moment whose water has broken, whose life is being born.

My seasons have a sacred strategy. Soon I will have this moment as memory. And I will be new. New and singing all the true notes of this life, my palatial life, rich in unforeseeable charity and fertile with fervent fields of Grace.

BE WILLING TO LET YOUR relationships change. Your relationships with your various ways of being. Breathe and release your lifestyle, habits, ideas, self-ideas, beliefs, emotional patterns, dreams, memories. Release what you have judged as bad or good. What is truly good for you will return to you. What was a harmful artifact of the world need not return.

Releasing all that you feel is essential to who you are can feel terrifying. Like the first moment when you jump off a cliff into the sea and your soul shifts in your chest and belly. Breathe past this first unsettling moment of releasing your relationship with ways of being, and you begin to feel a bright new sensation: transformation. Metamorphosis. This is what it feels like when wings are born.

WHY NOT TEAR UP your old contracts between you and you? Draw up new language that says *I choose peace. I choose peace. I choose peace...*

You can revise your life. It is not a stone certainty. More like a daily painting of Grace. Edit your inner agreements. You likely inherited them anyway. The authors before you were not original. They copied, too. Here's to the revisions that set you free. So many beautiful drafts ahead.

IF YOUR FLAWS and my flaws stood before God, Creator, Love, to be compared and judged, there would be no comparison. No judgment. God does not compare or judge flaws. God uses them. There is no flaw in that.

EVERY MOMENT has its sunrise, sun peak, and sunset. Its expression of Sacred Will. When we learn to move in this supernatural harmony and rhythm, we get the most out of life. We are preciously squeezing our moments. Fresh juice is produced. When we learn to make deep use of these seeds planted in us, we become a forceful garden. Fruitful. Fulfilled.

OUR LIFE IS NOT for our sake, but for the world's. The more efficient we are in harvesting what is planted in our moments, the more we have to share. The more plentiful our harvest, the more bountiful the meal of the masses. And in return, the more abundant our inner spring of daily Grace.

YOU ARE HERE, in this world, because you have been made to give. To open, part, and pour. To share, merge, and wed. To pollinate and flower. To increase the Light in all things. Keep learning your own way of moving inside the sunrise, sun peak, and sunset of your moments. This is how you grow your Peace.

KNOW WHEN to teach. And when to listen. So that through the example of your listening, you may teach.

WHEN A SQUIRREL prepares for winter, it is a prophet. A tree dropping its leaves is a prophet. A chick in a high nest, nervous before its first flight—a prophet. Lovers, opening their hearts for what's to come—paired prophets. Do not be exclusive, elitist, or prejudiced in presuming who is or is not a prophet. Prophets are everywhere.

YOU HAVE BEEN WORKING at this life of yours for a long time. How many promotions have you given yourself? Take the initiative and promote yourself to peace, self-kindness, self-forgiveness, and all you dream of. You deserve the raise.

I AM NOT THIS MOMENT. I am peace in this moment. I am not the turbulence of this time. I am peace and timeless. I am not this swirling, vining fear. I am peace, a sunlight ever near. I am not unwellness and ache. I am peace, a vibrant, crystal lake. I am not displaced. I am peace, a sacred land. I am not unsafe. I am peace, and well. I am not anxiety. I am peace, breathing freely in, out, releasing. Releasing everything.

I am life. I am prayer. I am ceremony. I am the masses. I am rare. I am poetry singing a sunrise song. I am dance. I am dream. I am memory. I am sage, sweetgrass, soil, drum, mountains rising, deep earth hum. I am generations. I am born for this day. I am alive in this day.

I am the soft serenade of winds of change. I am gentleness upon my own heart. My soul a drum. My spirit a drummer. My heart a Lover, forever in summer, who dances to the beat and rhythm of this moment. This moment, however it feels, is a purpose sweeping all the lands. And I. I am peace. A host for what arrives.

I open my heart, my soul, my life, and say *Welcome. Welcome, traveler. Come inside, sit, and rest. I will feed you, clothe you, shelter you, assure you. With this peace. I am.*

THERE IS AN OUTER SUN and an inner sun. We often seek the outer sun and grow dependent on the grace of weather. Neglecting our inner sun, which is always available, we grow unnecessarily dim and cold inside. Seeking to alleviate this suffering, we go on seeking the outer sun. Dear soul, you need not be vacant of warmth and light. Sit with your innerness. Behold the candlelight you are growing, casting illumination on your corners and crevasses. Behold your soul thawing into dance. Behold the centerpiece of your central peace. Behold the sun you are.

MAYBE YOU HAVE GROWN so accustomed to the old pain, you fear living without it. You do not believe in yourself without it. BeLoved, to realize this is the first step to freedom. If vines of pain have woven themselves through your architecture, the machete to unencumber yourself is the thought of you in no pain, repeated. Repeated until you experience yourself in no pain, in small, gaining moments of incredible time.

IMAGINE IF YOU REMEMBERED every good thing said about you the way you remember every bad thing said about you. Your relationship with yourself and life would be new. Good news. You can begin practicing today. Speak good things about you. Then remember. These are medicine ways. The wounds in you extend back to your ancestors. Touch the wounds. Touch your ancestors. Touch you.

LOOK AT YOU, setting boundaries. Acting like you want to be free. Setting boundaries does not make you mean. It makes you a custodian of your sacred life.

Boundaries are not walls that keep you in. They are windows that set you free. At first, you may feel guilty for not letting people take advantage of you any longer. As though their disappointment and hurt are more important than your wellness and freedom. Eventually you see the beauty and blessing in teaching people how to treat you. Those who care to honor this, stay. Those who never honored you to begin with, go. What remains is a life in which you feel honored. Especially by yourself. Nothing feels freer than that.

You will wish you had opened these windows to your sacredness long ago. For now, a modest first step. Say *No*. Say it without guilt or apology. Behold the life-changing power of saying *No* to what does not feel good for you, and *Yes* to what feels right for you. You are conditioning yourself for peace. Now is a divine springtime of your life. Open your many windows. Breathe a fresher air.

WHO SHALL BE your teachers today? They are all lined up and ready to share their lessons. They have done all the research, all the revisions and updates. Your teachers have been studying you all your life, learning how you learn, what your language is, and the way to your heart. No tuition. No keeping attendance. No grades or judgment. Just open yourself to your teachers. They are everything. Everywhere. Take delight in growing.

YOU DO NOT BECOME HAPPY. You remember happiness. Then, you resume the play. In some ways, happiness is a habit. An orientation of your mind and molecules toward joy. A joy unmoored from conditions. In other words, you say to yourself *In this moment, I choose to allow for happiness*. You repeat this choice, not forcing happiness, just allowing it to trickle and flow when it arises. You remove from your being the dam of reasons that hold back your aura of awe and wonder, of gratitude for your life.

Pain and sorrow are welcome in the house of true joy. The idea that they are not, cripples our relationship with joyfulness. Joy is not as extreme as we make it out to be. All your emotions can exist and be useful even within your personal culture of joyfulness. No need to be so hard on joy, so judgmental. Joy is not an emotion snob. It plays well with other emotions. Is suited for the streets just as well as for high society. When you encounter your own joy, do not ask *What is an emotion like you doing in a place like this?* Instead, say *It is good to see you here. Let's catch up on the good stuff.*

SOMETIMES, SILENCE is the song that most soothes your soul. Don't be afraid to play that music, too.

GRATITUDE DISSOLVES many sorrows. Life is not an entitlement. It is a miracle. Freedom for your soul begins with comprehending the soul of freedom: *Grace.*

THE WAY MORNING LIGHT feels to your soul. Study that lesson. Become a master. Be a living sunrise.

A BUTT-NAKED 1 year old is running wild through a room full of human rules and laws and customs, knocking everything over with the most precious joy and glee. Maybe, you should join the baby.

PEOPLE HAVE TAUGHT YOU to stifle the ocean of your tears into a meager trickle rarely released. But, beautiful soul, when you really feel something, it is good to be a river.

A SAFE, FREE RELATIONSHIP SPACE is like a wide open workshop for the soul. You can work on yourself there. We can spend many years in solitude *working on ourselves*. And yet, solitude can blind us to certain growth needs, just as relationships of any kind can. The blessing of a healthy relationship, platonic or not, is to offer us a compassionate mirror for the soul. A nurturing, safe, reflective presence we can look into and see ourselves in ways we wouldn't otherwise. Two people, when practicing sacredness with each other and themselves, can create a beautiful space together, a tender garden where what trembles in them can be held and soothed until it grows bold and burgeoning into the sky.

YOUR INNER STORIES have power. Examine them deeply so you are living an actual life, not just playing out played out stories.

YOUR ENTITLEMENT is to feel things. Your duty is to care for your feelings. On one end of the continuum is helplessness, the belief that you are at the mercy of your feelings. On the other end is the delusion of absolute control over your feelings. Both of these extremes leave you in a harmful relationship with your feelings. In between these two extremes is where you and your feelings can get down and get good. Your feelings want you to stop oppressing them, but also to not let them run all over you. Maybe, then, your feelings are like children. Give them freedom. Give them care. Love them even when they drive you crazy. They will grow up, become their true selves, and swell your life with meaning.

AN OCEAN of Love is in you. Don't swim in just a drop.

IF YOU COULD truly see the beauty of your soul, you would drop all your old, harmful ideas of you and fall in Love. You would be free. Your work in this life is to see your soul. So you may see the soul of the world. And bless the world of your soul. We don't need you to seek medicine. We need you to be medicine. Free, you are medicine for every soul.

EXPERIENCE YOUR own Love, which is collective Love. It will cure your loneliness, fear, and weariness, and revitalize your life. Soak in your entire Love ocean. Peace will bloom in parts of you that you didn't know existed. You don't have to be stuck in a tiny tide pool. You can feel the freedom of your boundless soul, a bliss greater even than you have dreamed.

IF YOU FEEL YOUR LIFE is lacking in miracles, maybe you weren't raised to see miracles. All of life is a miracle. Open your heavenly eyes.

Joy derives from wonder, which derives from being able to see the glory in wonderful things. Many with 20/20 vision are blind to sacred beauty. If you want to be filled with the grace of being all the away alive, practice seeing the often unseen essence of what life is offering: miracles in every moment. Seeing this is freedom.

YOU ARE NOT BROKEN, dear soul. Art is happening. Those cracks are how beauty births itself. They are the paintbrush. The paint. The painter. The painting. Behold your holy art.

WHEN IT FEELS as though the sun is crumbling, and your panic is a rising sea, return to your breathing. It is a messenger whispering *I was made for this. Even now, I am bliss.* You were made for this. Stay with your breathing. It is your medicine, home, peace sky, freedom.

ONE OF THE MOST powerful wellness practices is a deep, Loving breath. Its offspring shall be named *Peace*. And it shall populate your world.

CAN YOU LOOK through the muddy river water sediment of a person's social categories and labels and see their soul? Then you are medicine. Make your offering.

SHE INDULGED HERSELF with a Love letter. She wrote it in her journal while eating dark chocolate and drinking ginger lemonade. She wrote: *I want to be in bed with you watching a movie. Wake with you under a warm comforter of peace. Watch you move naked in space, in a poetry of silence. I want the sensation of unsensational things. The way earth and sky are with each other. Is how I want to make Love with you.*

YOUR SOUL'S FAVORITE food is peace. Eat plenty. There will always be leftovers. They taste better by the day.

CHERISH YOUR HEART. It is the only thing between you and a dispassionate life. You feel. Therefore you are. Hold sacred ceremonies daily in your heart. Your whole life happens there.

WHAT IS YOUR OFFERING? This is the sweet question of your life. Ask and answer as you go, evolving what you serve, as you heal and grow from being served. Dance light and limber in life's reciprocity. Taste all the fruit as you yourself sweeten into fruit for your offering. You are here for something. Live inside this something, and your wealth is a waterfall, your currency unconditional and composed of purpose-flowers and kinship breeze.

IF SOMEONE called you *Soul*, would you answer? Know who and what you are. Everything will flow. We exist not according to our circumstance, but according to our idea of who and what we are. Align your nature and calling with your identity, and you shall have a life of abundant grace in an atmosphere of peace.

YOU HAVE NOT BEGUN to see the profound beauty of your soul. Keep opening your eyes. For the rest of your life, keep opening your eyes. You have not yet achieved your clearest vision. This path is worth the walking. As you see your soul beauty, you see the soul of Beauty. Which is life.

YES. YOU ARE THAT WORTHY. Of what? Everything good. Is this your answer when you pose the question to yourself? If it is not, then, dear one, you know where to do your private work. You are worthy of everything good. Let this truth seep down into you and become the honest story of who you are: an embodiment of worthiness. Not perfect or constant in feeling worthy. Just consistent enough that your life looks like a home where someone worthy lives.

DO NOT WORRY whether the glass is half full or half empty. Concern yourself with what is in the glass. What purpose is in the glass of this moment, dear soul? That is the question. Breathe beautifully and contemplate what this moment means for you. For the world. Filled with Grace, begin planting. This is a planting season. Soon the glorious harvest. What are your divine crops?

DO NOT ABANDON Love. Not now. Not ever. Love is a spirit of caring. Its blood type is (H)ope. Love's caring spirit keeps you in the world, keeps the world in you. Fear, ugliness, and suffering seduce you: *Come with us. Leave Love behind.* Reject those false flowers. When life quakes and it feels all of Creation is teetering, do not abandon Love. It is your way through. Love is the life in the life of your life.

No abandones el Amor. Ahora no. Nunca. El Amor es un espíritu de cariño. Su tipo de sangre es Esperanza. El espíritu cariñoso del Amor te mantiene en el mundo, mantiene el mundo en ti. El miedo, la fealdad y el sufrimiento te seducen: *Ven con nosotros. Deja atrás el*

Amor. Rechaza esas flores farsantes. Cuando la vida tiembla y se siente que toda la Creación se tambalea, no abandones el Amor. Es tu camino a través. El Amor es la vida en la vida de tu vida.

IT IS NOT THAT your fear is unreasonable, dear soul. It is that it is unfruitful. Give yourself permission to plant and grow fruit trees of the mind. For your beautiful life, you need roots of faith and courage that are stronger than your fear. Boil each down to their essence and drink them. This is how you will know which is the stronger brew.

PEOPLE SAY they want to grow old together. Old ones know the secret: Grow young together.

WHEN YOU CARESS a living thing, it heals and grows. Your heart. A Lover. The world.

THERE ARE THINGS that are not real, which we treat as though they are everything. And things that are everything that we treat as though they are not real. This is how we weave our pain and confusion. You know what to do: Unweave these delusions and illusions. Grow still. Recognize sacredness. Touch it with Love. Weave it through and through.

WHAT YOU TELL yourself in the worst of times becomes your mantra in the best of times. Your stories make your life. Practice deepening their roots in times of peace. In times of trouble, deepen your practice.

TAKE CLOSE CARE of your inner stories. They create your outer life. Reality isn't your biggest threat. Your inner stories about reality are. People say *I have trouble sleeping*. What they really mean is *I have trouble storying*. Our story creates our condition. The best time to examine, mend, and reweave your stories is all the time. Do it when you are awake, so you dream better in your sleep. Do it when you sleep, so you live better when you are awake.

When life grows daunting, get down with your stories and spend special time. If you neglect your stories, they fray and turn against you. If you nurture your stories, they carry you through the worst, and bring you all the way to a paradise called *Peace* in a land called *Freedom*.

Gather with your people however you can and share your sacred stories. The ancestral ones that keep you well. We are not only living through the season of our circumstances. We also are journeying through our stories. Our healthy stories are water in the desert. *Drink*. Hope in the valley. *Graze*. Mountains in the mist. *Climb*. Medicine for our memory. *Pour*. Manna for the masses. *Share all the food. Let your people feast.*

TOUCH. YOUR. PEACE. It needs you now. Your plants, pets, and people all respond to your Loving touch. So does your peace. Peace is a living thing. It needs your attention and care. Touch it with deep breathing, prayer, praise, song, stillness, silence, servitude, art, dance, movement, mantra, rest, romance, release, relationship with your various soul nutrients. To stay free you require staying in touch with your peace. It is a wonderful presence inside you. A shimmering, sacred lake. To wake it, touch the water.

IF YOU MUST call yourself something, call yourself a Lover. If you must name this day, name it a gift. If you must label your pain, label it a window. If you must title your purpose, title it Divine.

SO MUCH YOU cannot control. But you can control your breathing. Can you breathe a moment of peace into your soul? Start there. If you don't know where to start, or how to get from one moment to the next, start with a single, beautiful breath. Then another. String them together. Peace is the fruit of what you practice. Sweet dreams, sweet soul.

HOME WORKOUT: *Deep breath. Repeat.* Soul care: *Deep breath. Repeat.* Bedtime: *Deep breath. Repeat.* Deep breathing directly boosts your immune system. It also floods your brain and body with peace chemicals. Get your reps in as you go through the day. And make deep breathing your bedtime story. Bless your sleep.

IF YOU DO NOT FEEL WORTHY of sending Love, you will not send it. If you do not feel worthy of receiving Love, you will not receive it. Loving is not a matter of deciding to engage in Love. It is a matter of self-worth. This is the garden inside that needs your healing touch.

HOLD ONTO YOUR JOY. Dearly hold onto your joy. It is a flotation device when the waters get rough. You have every right to seek and savor joy in challenging times. Joy is best practice. Salvation mode. Chosen resistance act. Proclamation of enduring life. If you look closely, you may see reasons for joy where you did not before. Quietude and stillness have a way of shining a light on the littlest of blessings. Which are not little at all. Dear soul, I hope you will take your daily dose of joy. Double your dose if you need.

SOLITUDE IS LIKE a friendly dog. You can touch it. It won't bite. Go ahead, dear soul. Touch it. You may fear solitude, but it does not fear you. It wants to Love you. Show you things about yourself. About this world. About life. It wants to take you out on long walks through the wilderness of your soul. Acquaint you with the wonders of your spirit. Reintroduce you to your true self. Solitude is a divine music. If you open to it, it can stir irresistible movement in you. It can make your whole existence dance.

WHEN YOU FEEL a moment of clear peace, archive this feeling. So you can repost it in your heart. Live stream peace. Feel peace. Archive peace. Repost peace. Remix and re-release peace.

ODE TO TENDERNESS...

You giant wave of feeling. Always in need of a soul caress. Your heart is like April. Beauty blooming everywhere. Pollen of pain and pleasure coming and going, lifting and dropping. Sometimes you need the solace of a sip of rain. A soft button of water on a small leaf. So much grief. Waves and waves of what washes through this world. Pouring through you. Soaking your bones. Staining your blood in turquoise melancholy.

You are puddle after puddle of Love. Mud puddles. Clear puddles. Paradises of pooled emotion. You felt that cloud in the sky. Last year. You felt it. A thousand miles from you. But you felt it. You rained inside. You comforted that cloud. It smiled as it drifted away from you. Grateful.

Forests on the other side of earth are a braille of feeling that you read in your chest as prophecy and praise. Sometimes your pillow is your pastor. It catches your confessions and tears. Becomes a warm lake in which you bathe your sonnet face. Your Grace keeps you feeling all these souls. All these living things.

And your heart. Your heart is the sand at the mercy of these giant waves of feeling. Your heart is a mountain, towering over those who do not feel, choose not to feel, run from feelings, tame their feelings, dilute their feelings. Your heart is a mountain. A sky. A universal womb. You gestate our collective feelings.

Inner peace is a butterfly you chase, though it is in truth a butterfly already inside you, dancing lightly on the flowers of your spirit meadow. You are on your back gazing a blue sky of feeling. Meadow hums with industry of little living things lit with the emotions of being alive. You translate their chorus. Your heart is a ministry. A scripture of sensitivity. A kind conversation in a sanctuary of feeling. And you want to be touched.

Everywhere in you aches. You want your own touch, if only you can find the right touch. You want the touch of others, if only they can find the right touch. You want your hurt to be untouched. You tell yourself you have been touched too much. You pray for a touch of peace.

You have moments when you curse your tenderness. Moments when you want these waves of worldly feeling to pause, to evaporate. Yet you know your tenderness is keeping you alive. If you closed its door, you would have no more passage to your days of meaning. No more communion with Glory. So you leave open wide the door. And sun showers come through. And breeze parades into your heart with a message: *This life will always touch your tenderness. And your tenderness will always touch this life. Your tenderness is the divine artist. This world is its miraculous art.*

And you, you in your throbbing, pulsing, aching, laughing, crying, dancing ceremony of tenderness are the open prairie, the wide wilderness through which this song of life finds its notes and vessel. You giant wave of feeling.

You are here to give us a soul. A soul like April. Beauty blooming everywhere.

FREEDOM IS NOT doing whatever you want to do. Freedom is existing in a simultaneous condition of not oppressing and not being oppressed. This is a rare sky. Many never take flight in this sky. Some taste its exquisite air briefly, in scattershot bursts of moments. Very few souls are able to stay aloft in freedom's sky. They are the ones who are willing to die on the anvil of humility, to fall off the mountain endlessly, and endure a new climb. They give their lives to this sacred practice, this sacrificing of convenience to engender the inner and outer streams of peace. They are freedom in human form. You were born with the nature to be one of them. Yes. You were.

WE HAVE ALL WALKED through the lonesome, painful lands of our past imperfections. Share your life with those who do not make you stay in those lands repenting, but instead walk with you without judgment through the bright valley of your healing and growing. Stay close to the ones who only care to see the person you are now, and the person your soul whispers of becoming.

ASK ANY MOTHER who has been through it. Birthing new life breaks you as it blesses you. Welcome to the delivery room that is your *Now*. No matter the pain of this moment, know it is a sacred moment. Treat it sacredly. If you don't know how to exist sacredly, that's what this birthing is for.

DEAR REVOLUTIONARY: You are tired. Do not accept the toxic, dehumanizing idea that this is no time for rest. For a revolutionary, every moment is a time for rest. With each deep, Loving breath, thought, and feeling, restore yourself. This is how you keep your revolution alive.

Some people misunderstand a revolution as a spirit of anger and rage. If it were, it would die quickly. A true revolution is a spirit of sacred Love. A people's Love for themselves. This is why a revolution is born, lives long, and prospers. Because it is a deeply Loved offspring.

Some say *This is not a time for rest. It is a time to amplify.* This mentality is a reflection of the colonizing grind culture that damaged, destroyed, and enslaved us all in the first place. Reject your oppressor's poison. Drink your own organic juice: wellness. Rest is sacred. It is vital. It is non-negotiable.

No longer think of rest as a long departure from more important work. Think of it as an integrated, continuous return to your deepest work: being all the way alive. The eternal ones understand this and whisper to us now: *Children, in every moment, no matter what you face, you can heal yourself with rest.*

Rest is a life skill. When you master it, you realize it is not a departure from your life. It is the soul of your life. A nurturing you do in the garden of each precious breath and moment. *Freedom.*

DEAR REVOLUTIONARY: Your whole life has prepared you for this moment. Have faith in your journey. You were born for this era on earth. The old, sick world is dying. A new world emerges through the birth canal of a vast healing. You are the medicine. The midwife. The mourning. The morning. No matter how terrifying the moments to come, no matter how towering the mountain, know that this is your destiny. No other moment. This one. Call on all the people of all your people. Hold the circle. Rise. Birth this paradise.

MAYBE YOU FEEL the revolution does not need you. Come. Bring everything. Bring the ocean. Bring the sky. Bring all the stars of all the galaxies. Bring the very sediment of your soul. Freedom needs you. Freedom is not yet free.

IF YOU ARE A LIVING THING, you are culpable in the fate of living things. If you do not feel culpable, you have not learned the grace of humility, a spirit that binds us not only to each other but also to that pristine standard of Sacredness.

If you do not recognize your own suffering as a thread in the weaving of all suffering, your own soul is in jeopardy. This dawn now upon us is not a time for you to separate yourself as a pure and superior savior. Now is the time for you in your idea of yourself to rejoin the blemished, ever pollutable soil of what it means to be human.

If you cannot feel the suffering of others, likely you cannot truly feel your own suffering. Nor, therefore, can you recognize your profound and pervasive unwellness and the terror it rains upon the world.

These are not words of assault or to extract guilt. These words are how Love urges you to do the labor, yours and yours alone, to Heal. Your. Soul. And be Love in a world that cannot bear you being other than a note in the ancient spiritual song that cries *freedom*.

A PRAYER. That you may live in your truth. And receive its blessings. That we may live in our collective truth. And reap its generations of Grace. If the mountain between denial and truth is towering, we must climb it. If the ocean between sickness and healing is boundless, we must swim it. We must find the will and the way to kill our deadly fairytales and fables and grow lungs for breathing and living inside the truth of who we are. It is the only way to reach who we want to be.

You have to admit you are unwell if you want to romance wellness. Pain erupted in the world is not a sign of wellness. It is the suffering wail of unwellness calling out to its mother: wellness. It wants to come home.

IS IT YOUR HABIT to say you don't have time for wellness? Maybe, dear one, your inner story is the perfect host for your unwellness. If you want a better guest, extend a more appealing invitation. Wellness will arrive.

TIME IS A PERVASIVE, oppressive colonial violence. When the clock says *Time's up*, whatever you were doing to heal and feed your soul is abruptly ended: Making Love. Tender touching. Sensitive listening, speaking. Being with sunrise. Sleep. Eating. Learning. Crying. Grieving. Gestating. Birthing. All of it. Violently ended.

Even the way you moved through those moments was polluted by your anxiety about the time ending. Our abrupt starting and stopping of moments is killing us. We are literally starting and stopping our souls. This is trauma. In the Indigenous worlds before colonialism, time did not exist. Moments did. And we were whole and free in our moments. And our moments were whole and free in us.

We can reclaim our timeless life, enrich our moments and health, and release our anxious, soul-depleting attachment to a fabricated construct. Our healing practice involves learning to be fully present, paying attention to our time dependencies, and gradually reshaping our lives to be liberated from the tyranny of fractional time. We can be free again.

GRATITUDE IS A RIVER. If you live in it, your heart and soul grow supple. You flow with life. If you leave gratitude's river behind, everything you are grows hard, rigid, suffering. Your body, your spirit, your relations, your life.

Stay in the river, Revolutionary. Especially as you work to heal and unpeel the countless layers of oppression that shape your life and the world. Identify your blessings. Name them, so they know when you are calling for them. Feed them. They like organic nourishment. Praise them. They will swell. Mantra their names. They will multiply. Rest with them. They will be your shade tree and blanket. Sing to them. They will be your fire and dance. Stay in the river of Gratitude. It will carry you to your dream home. Which is Peace.

LOVE LIKE LOVE LOVES. And how does Love love? Without condition. For humans, this is the most difficult way of Love to follow. But Love does not like, enable, or forget. Love loves. Love loves boundlessly, brilliantly, boldly. Subtly and seeping. Sublime and soundless.

Love loves enduringly. Hopefully. Faithfully. Fearlessly. Privately. Publicly. With Grace. Not seeking glory. Love weaves blankets and baskets of the past, present, and future. Blankets that hold and do not fray. Love appraises you and finds you worthy. Love speaks the truth. Is not always polite. Does not consider comfort. Love obliterates ego and myth.

What Love touches heals. What Love reaches feels. What Love bows to kneels. Love glances at sewage and turns it sacred. Love changes slander to praise. Love is a sacred storyteller. Love destroys all castles, drains all moats, rubbles royalty and thrones. Love answers. Prayers. Poetry. Passion fires. Love revolts.

Love constantly births. Lets go. Remembers. Wakes your embers. Love is not romantic blindness. It is searing vision. Love sees. Love kills what is already dying, diseased, polluted, corrupted. Love makes all things new. Love is not in you. You are in Love. And all of this is Love.

HERE IS WHAT WE do know. Your soul is beautiful. And deserves to be free. Imagine the effort a butterfly endures to break free from the chrysalis. Imagine the suffocating entrapment. The determination and will. Imagine that first free breath. Imagine the infinite sky. And a lifetime of flying. Our world is straining to break free from the chrysalis of centuries of sick oppression. And you, dear soul, need to do what it takes in your life, in your being, to finally... feel... your glorious wings... drafting Freedom's sky.

WHO REMINDS YOU of God, Creator, Sacredness, Divine? Let them move your soul. Often, in nature, plants and animals give off chemicals to protect them from what they sense is a threat. They do the same to attract what they sense is good for them. The soul knows. Then it informs the body. Consult your soul for what moves it. Move toward that.

IN TIMES OF BOTH PERSONAL and collective suffering, sometimes the medicine is sweet. Often it is bitter. But if the medicine finally cures you and ends your suffering, you forget all about the taste of the medicine. You are too busy singing its praises. Truth is our medicine today. May we take it.

IT IS QUITE POSSIBLE, you brilliant seamstress of dreams, that what you are weaving in this moment is the fabric of peace that will clothe you for the rest of your life. Tend to your threads.

BETWEEN THE FIRST and last heartbeat of your day, you will tell a thousand stories to the audience that is your soul. Make sure your stories give life to your life. Speak medicine. Your life is a storytelling convention. Peace lives in the words. Rest well. Cut the kite strings on your worries. Let the wind have them. Let yourself have this moment of unrepeatable Grace.

EVEN YOUR PAIN is a messenger from Love. A kindness pointing you toward healing and peace. Don't pack your bags. Leave behind what you've known. You'll not be coming back this way again. Your pain is a sacred land. Not to live in. To journey through. Keep bravely moving. Only you can cross this mystic territory. What a gift.

BABIES DON'T SUCKLE because they calculate the odds of receiving milk. They suckle because it is innate to their essential need. It does not occur to them that something they need so badly might not be provided. Live your whole life like this.

YOU HAVE TO FEED the past, or it will grow ravenous and come for you. You feed the past by honoring it. By carrying forth its lessons, wisdoms, pain, and beauty. Treat it not as a thing to be discarded, but as the old growth forest that oxygenates your current life and protects life in the future. Feed the past by talking story with it. Display its art in your modern galleries. Thank it for the meaning it offers you, and for the path it hewed on which you now travel.

Only greed and conquest cultures devalue and dishonor the past. They know the past is where their guilt, shame, and reckoning are rooted. They avoid the true past even if it kills them. To have a strong relationship with the true past is to have a conscience. Greed and conquest cannot bear to have a conscience. But you can. Be in relation with what has been, so you can be at peace with what is now. In you. In everything.

JUST MAYBE, if you call your pain a friend, it will speak to you more Lovingly. It may even let you go. And if the idea of healing your pain feels like a grain of sand at the foot of an impossible mountain, try to remember: Single drops of rain can turn mountains into grains of sand.

BELOVED. May you *feel* better. Not as in your health or mood improving. But as in growing in the way you feel. May you feel in a better way. A way that heals you and brings you home to the truth you are. May you feel the way living things feel. Without ego, denial, false stories, fleeing, or judgment. May you purely, entirely feel. This is how you release your feelings. By feeling them deeply. With Love. Your feelings want you to touch them. Then they will let you be. So you may have room for more pure feeling. If you *feel* better, you will feel better. Feel this?

MAYBE SAY *I Love you* more often. To you. Water your heart devotedly. Watch it bloom.

YOU SEE IN the world so many wonders and miracles. Make sure you see the wonder and miracle you are. Recognize the profound happening that is your life.

YOUR SOUL IS a scripture. Listen to its sacred words. Have faith in your true voice and presence: your soul. It knows the way. It will see you through.

THAT WASN'T FEAR you just felt. It was the feeling of your soul saying *I want freedom.*

WHEN YOU QUESTION what will become of the world, try to remember, *you* are what will become of the world. And you have a say in that.

Revolution is not a matter of if or when. It is a matter of what we are willing to endure in the absence of revolution. When that point is breached, by whatever means or moment, we behold the striking of an irrepressible fire.

Sometimes, after 400, 500 years, the collective human soul rises up and regurgitates all the poison it has swallowed. When that tidal wave breaks upon the common shores of norm and complacency, all that matters for each of us are these sacred questions:

Do I choose now to become an ancestor worthy of this life I have been given? Am I willing to add my flame to the fire? Am I a living thing? Do living things count me as one of them?

YOUR HEART FEELS it all. Your spirit feels it all. Your mind thinks it all. Your body stores it all. You are birthing a whole new world. That is why you feel this way. You are doing just fine. Go easy.

Yes. You are that powerful. As you change, let go, and heal, you change and heal the world. As you envision and dare a new world inside you, you birth a new world all around you.

This moment is not a wait and see. It is a seeing. No more waiting. Your time is now. Not an urgent now. A patient, gentle season of now. Breathe beautifully. You are about to change forever. We bow now to your brave revolution of the soul.

WE SAY WE FEEL THINGS in the heart. First, we feel things in the soul. The heart translates that into emotion. Your soul is feeling now. Hold it closely. Tell it sweet stories. Feed it a serving of hope and peace.

SHE WAS NOT JUST TIRED. She was uninspired. She traced back the path she had taken since birth and realized it was a path laid down by others. She left the path. Stepped where there were no footprints. Learned to make choices that pleased her soul. She felt something new and wonderful grow in her chest. She came to call this feeling Peace.

I hope you are finding ways to breathe *in spite of*, you sacred river stone. What you can control is how you sustain your wellness as you move through life's turbulence and swells. You are worthy of that Grace.

We inhabit freedom through our wellness. Nourish yourself with whatever nourishes you. Weave togetherness with all your relations, all your ancestors, all who cherish your vitality. True life Loves you and is with you. No matter what comes, you are walking the sacred path of your singular soul. This is a choosing and a collective medicine all at once. All our relations.

OF COURSE YOUR FEELINGS rise and fall. You are made of water and waves. Motion and music. Living things go to the water to drink, cleanse, find peace. Be with your water. Feel your moments. Let the feelings bless you with their messages. Then set them free.

ALLOWING HERSELF TO BE IMPERFECT was one of the kindest things she had ever done. For anyone. It did not just change her life. It changed her aura. Which changed everyone in her life.

PRECIOUS CHILD ASKED Grandmother: *What does it mean to reweave your life?*

Grandmother answered: *Unlearn your old harmful ways. Learn your new healing ways. Garden the stories you tell yourself. Allow beauty to run like a river through your soul again. Permit peace to graze your heart. Drink the rain. Savor the sun. Love like Love loves.*

DEAR SOUL. Your life is a sacred blanket. Some of its threads are meant to unravel, fall away. You may replace them with new threads glistening with the breaching sunlight of your nascent knowing, supple with the dew of your dawning season.

To take hold of the high fruit you need now, you must let go your grasp on the old ways that brought you here. Do not be afraid to drop your leaves when a foretelling chill touches your tenderness. Nakedness precedes the lushness of bloom.

Breathe beautifully now. With a blush of Grace. You are not lost. You are coming home. Even in the seeming chaos, even in the wailing wilderness, your soul is a native species in the territory of your lifetime. You belong. You are a dream, a cascading brilliance. *Shonto.* Light that shines on Spirit water. Breathe beautifully now. *Osiyo.* It is true and good.

IF YOU FIND YOURSELF feeling like a wilted plant, maybe that is a Loving sign. Water your soul. Your soul is very Loving to you. Even after years of neglect, it trusts you. It opens up and lets you know how it is feeling, and what it needs. Pay caring attention to what it expresses, how it feels about how you feed and water it. It will let you know its current mood, craving, and appetite.

Your soul does not often call for grandiose nurturing. Simple, subtle servings suffice. If you feel wilted, that is your soul tenderly, patiently letting you know its condition and what it needs. Slow and still yourself enough to hear this divine conversation. You can restore your greater glory. Big beautiful breaths... water your soul.

YOU ARE NOT ONLY feeling *your* life. You are feeling all life. At all times. This is so much feeling to feel. Rest. Renew. Nurture your phenomenal heart.

LIFE IS AN ETERNAL springtime. If you are alive, this is your season to bloom.

IF YOU CAN take a deep, releasing breath, you have just Loved yourself.

HAVE YOU MET yourself? It could change your life. Take the time. Go inside. Make your closest friend. Learning how to truly, fully be with yourself is one of the greatest gifts you can give yourself and all the souls touched by your *homefulness*. When you know yourself, peace becomes probable. Your aura takes on the essence of harmony between who you are and how you live. Learn to be at home in your soul. Like all other nourishing things, it is a practice. You are divinely equipped for the relationship.

ARE YOU STILL WONDERING if the world needs your offering? You didn't bake the bread. You are the bread the Baker prepared. Let yourself be served. Don't worry about whether you are ready. Your blessings have been readied for you. You aren't the baker of the blessings. You are the bread your blessings are here to bake.

LET'S HEAL TOGETHER. The best kind of proposal.

SELF-CENTEREDNESS amplifies inner suffering, which in turn creates more self-centeredness. Servitude heals the root of personal pain by touching the seed of that pain: your own Loving nature. You were not just hurt. Your Loving nature was hurt. Servitude allows you to nurse your Loving nature back into its wholeness by engaging it out in the world. In service to others. In service to Life.

Serve and you become less self-centered and therefore less consumed in your hurt. Allow your hurt to flow and circulate itself out of you, into the dissipating breath of your own compassion. Compassion readjusts your identity from *I* back to *We*. This creates open windows through which your hurt can release from you out into the sky. Serve others and you soothe your suffering, which leaves you in a mood and condition to serve some more.

A HAWK in the sky does not question flight. It flies. You are alive. Don't question your living. Live.

SOULFUL SILENCE is a sacred medicine blanket. Wrap yourself in it, daily. It will keep you warm.

WHISPER LOVE. Quell gossip. Sing praise.

OPEN YOUR HEART even wider. You have yet to know the paradise that is your infinite Love territory.

IF YOU KNEW paradise was just outside your door, would you only crack open the door? Open wide your heart.

WHEN YOU ARE true to you, you give us music we have never heard before. Do not deprive our virgin ears.

YOU DO NOT HAVE TO follow the herd in your spiritual questing. Your soul has its own appetite and grace.

LISTEN MORE closely to what life is whispering to you. A song is in the whisper that can set you free.

THE WATERS MAY FEEL rough right now. We are each rowing this boat with the oars we have been given. Do not judge. Not even yourself. Especially not yourself. You do not have to be heroic, grind yourself to death, have a life-changing revelation, discover a world-saving cure, sacrifice your soul, be grim or solemn, or drown in social causes. You can curl up under a blanket, hold your heart like a baby, just be with yourself tenderly, and still be a wonderful and worthy person. Worthy of what? Worthy of Love. And if you are worthy of Love, you are worthy of all good things.

SAY THESE WORDS: *I am not a brand. I am a life. My words are not content or quotes. They are my soul. I am not grinding. I am growing, grooving, grounded in glory. I have no followers. Only flowers that lean toward the sun that is my Love, which is not only my Love. Love is sovereign. We are its flute.*

It is possible to reject this soulless modern culture and offer to yourself and the world something of the substance of your own soul. Be sacred. Give yourself permission. Infuse your life with the incense and fragrance of authenticity. Purity of motive. Grandeur of servitude. Do not fear being a deep, meaningful, textured, naked, tear-soaked, rapturous, profoundly singular thing. We need this from you: More than a lifelong advertisement in human form. Rather, an actual human. Being.

IF YOUR FREEDOM oppresses others, it is not freedom. It is personal convenience. Many like the idea of freedom, but not its actual conditions. Self-centeredness is not the path to freedom. Dissolution into all things is the path to freedom. When the self becomes a sun inside all things, and all things rejoice inside the solar self, you are free.

Freedom is the perfume of unconditional, boundless Love. Become a connoisseur of the scent.

STAY IN YOUR wilderness. That's where your soul grazes. Feed yourself moonlight, wildflowers, and rebellion tea.

TONIGHT, MOON WILL DO THINGS to the night that make souls sigh in wonder and awe. Your dreams, too, are a moon. Let them glow. Tonight moon will do things that make sky blush. Be like the moon to your own heart.

Make your inner sky glow. Bubble bath. Candlelight. Beautiful breathing. Releasing. Remembering. Sing. Cry. Laugh. Dance. Drum. Stay in ceremony. Talk story. Journal your soul. Eat in a good way. Make Love. Dream bold. Entertain your ancestors. Behold your life. Feel awe at your many miracles. Shake your bones loose of old worries that don't belong in your new day.

Say. *I am moon. I sip sunlight like sangria. I seduce the tides. I am alive in this world. This world is alive in me. I am moon. Beadwork of brilliance. A phenomenon of boundless grace, performing peace.*

YOUR MIND NEEDS Love, too. Send it a fresh bouquet: your deep, peace-soaked breathing. When your mind receives flowers like this, its only thought is, *I really am safe and cared for*. That is when your mind starts putting out the good stuff. That is when your life starts living.

THE EARTH CULTURE people celebrated themselves so passionately because they knew: You cannot survive genocide if you do not Love yourself with a righteous fire.

YOU ARE ALL THE GLORIOUS GLIMPSES you have ever gathered of your soul. All of them. They are not separate creatures. They are one. Your soul. Is. Priceless. No matter what.

Freedom is not something you weigh on a scale. It is your ability to see yourself clearly, and therefore to see all of which you are a part. Freedom is a recognition, a remembrance that activates your sacred life.

SOME PEOPLE get confused and believe your life is their possession to dictate and direct. Walk on. Wild and free.

WHEN PEOPLE are used to looking down at you, it can cause a pain in their ego to look up at you. Make them learn a new yoga pose: *humble human*. Do not feed people's supremacy sickness. Starve that virus by living whole and free.

YOU MAY NOT FEEL READY for this season of your life. Worry not. This season of your life is ready for you. Know this, dear soul. A place has been prepared for you in the season now upon you. You are the honored guest. Even if you do not realize it, you have been prepared for this time and circumstance. If you were not prepared, the season would not have arrived. Soul seasons do not follow your calendar. They follow your soul. Where you are tender, pour some Love on it and proceed. Your season is here and it wants you. Want it back. That is the signal that brings forth its fruit.

TREATING YOURSELF SACREDLY SHOULD BE your most passionate revolution. Revolutionary work is rooted inside the soul. That is where freedom grows.

TREAT A PERSON for who they are, not as a dumping ground for your hurt from others. Yes, this is of course easier said than done. This doesn't mean it is impossible. We are talking about a personal commitment to take imperfect yet devoted care with our pain.

Carrying water up from the river to the village, it sloshes up out of the container. We do not surrender to the sloshing. We slow down. Take a deep breath. We take more care.

Our pain, when cared for, can become medicine. When we let it slosh all over others who have not harmed us, now our pain is a paradise lost, a greater suffering found. Also, you yourself are not a dumping ground, not even for your own hurt. Take care with your inward sloshing of that water, too.

THE FIRST THING exhausted people tell you is *I don't have time to rest*. The first thing rested people tell you is *I invest my sacred time in rest*. What is your *restimonial*?

PERHAPS IT IS the negative idea of suffering that this culture conditions us to that causes you now to wonder about the embracing of suffering. Many other cultures view suffering as a compassionate blessing. A gift of things dying in us so that new aspects in us may be born and live. Suffering is not easy or comfortable. This does not mean it is bad. When you were born, you suffered. When you exercise, you suffer. When flowers bloom they suffer. It takes great energy and will to open to the sun.

And if we only tolerate suffering rather than opening to it (embracing), we may not receive all the blessings it has for us. Suffering has a way of making us see what is real. What matters. It strips away our focus on frivolous things. This does not mean we should seek suffering. That idea is a self-destructive confusion.

When suffering arrives, we can invite it to sit with us and tell us its best stories, the stories we need at the time. Life is not about the absence of suffering. It is about the meaning we gather whatever our condition, suffering or not. We can embrace the harvest and our gathering of it. Or we can resent and run from the crop.

YOUR SOUL IS full because you are *soul-full*. Grant yourself your actual nature. You never were the shallow end of the pool. Feel what you feel and hold it like a newborn baby. Let your soul be swaddled.

WE ARE GROWN UP now, playing grown up games. But we have child hearts and hurts and fears, and want to be Loved and reassured and belong, all the same. We suffer most of all as adults because we believe we have outgrown our childhood needs. So we suppress them. We deny and oppress them. We try to be hard when in our deepest places we are so very tender.

Grown folks who heal deeply surrender to the truth that we will always be children at heart. Those needs never go away. Practice releasing your shame about needing now what you needed then. Your nature does not change. Your ability to honor and nurture your nature can change. Your true needs are not childish. They are childlike. As you learn the difference you begin to grow gentle with yourself. At last, a safe space for you. In you. I Love you.

YOUR SOUL is a precious pearl I want to polish in the unabbreviated ocean of my Love.

TO BE A HUMAN being in the eyes of human beings, you must act against the genocide of human beings. This is the sacred law.

IT'S CALLED OUTRAGE, not *Inrage*. You are supposed to let it out. Find your sacred ways.

THE EASIEST destination to reach when the world boils over is illness. Out of all the things they have taken from you, do not let them take your health. Keep that. So you have something to give to those who Love you.

WHEN YOU SEE the miracles in every moment, you flood your heart with awe, thanks, and praise. Worry dissolves. Fear fades away, replaced by glory rays. Sing. Sing praise.

WHEN YOU LEARN to cherish yourself, your life is no longer consumed with needful longing. Instead it is awash in joyful contentment and all the divine spices of Peace.

IF YOU ARE GOING to feel deep as the ocean, it may help to breathe as big as the sky.

To say life is turbulent right now is like saying the ocean is similar to a bathtub. Feeling deeply is not problematic. Not supporting your deep feeling is where the problems come. You can find endless ways to breathe that don't involve your lungs. Give yourself permission to breathe in all the creative, soulful ways that help you release your ocean. Big sky breaths. This is how we move through this time on earth. In a culture enamored with hoarding, may you fall in Love with releasing. May it be a wonderful practice in your life.

WHETHER YOU CALL YOUR LOVE Reiki, Allah, Dance, Compassion, Christ, Buddha, Mercy, Empathy, Crystals, Channeling, Ra, Passion, Kindness, or Grace, just make sure it is truly Love.

WHOEVER YOU ARE and whoever I am, our traumas are just getting acquainted. Let's be gentle with each other.

WE ARE NOT INVINCIBLE, untouched things. Like nubile sprouts in a turbulent garden, we are an aching world of tenderness. May we touch accordingly. How would you caress a raindrop? Start like that.

TEARS, LIKE RAINFALL, are a softening agent. Use them when the pain is hard. They are a renewable resource. Use them freely. Soak in them if you need to. Splurge.

GATHER ALL YOUR OLD STORIES that hold you down and back. Hold a ceremony and let them go. Begin weaving new stories of healing, beauty, and possibility. Your life is not a thing that happens. It is a story you tell, and from the telling, your journey is born and lives.

I WISH YOU would just Love and accept me as I am. Says your soul to you every moment of your life.

SO MANY FALSE STORIES told to us. So many we tell ourselves. Buried beneath it all is your true soul. To Love your soul is an *unburial*. An excavation. A shedding of ideas and identities. Mantras can remove this infertile sediment that suffocates your native song. Find your medicine words, dear soul. Repeat them until you can feel the sky of your true nature kissing your face. Keep going. Never stop lifting the veil. Never stop washing your spirit clean. Big Love.

LOOK UPON A THING and call it sacred. Touch a thing and call it sacred. Hear a thing and call it sacred. Feel a thing and call it sacred. Remember, dream, dance, sing, cry, laugh, and call it sacred. Behold yourself and call it sacred. This is how you mend your soul and the world.

WE, THE WORLD, suffer not from a lack of knowledge. We suffer from a lack of sacredness in our way of life. We desecrate everything. Especially our own precious self. Desecrated things suffer and bring suffering. We heal by relearning sacredness.

TOUCH SACREDLY what is tender in you. See it transform at the anointing of your Love. This is how powerful you are. You make what is weary and worn a Grace renewed.

IF YOU COULD hold in your hands all the stories you have ever told yourself, how many would be true? Would your hands overflow with true stories or would they be nearly empty of those? Examine your stories, dear soul. Healing lives inside what you find.

YOU CANNOT stand high atop a mountain of suffering souls and proclaim yourself free. Freedom is not an individual condition. It is a collective caring. A sustained devotion. A subtle symphony of interwoven soulfulness. Freedom weeps.

ASSUME EVERYONE you meet is having a hard time. It helps to wake your compassion.

If you are going to presume, presume to Love. Train your heart into this habit, and your soul will be blessed immeasurably. If we assume collective tenderness is our human condition, perhaps we will open our hearts to the truth of tenderness. Perhaps we will sing Mercy, not malice. Hardness and harshness are obsolete. They do not serve this new world being born. Ask yourself: What do mothers and babies need to thrive through the moment of birth? Give yourself and the world the same Grace. Ego says *Fortify the castle*. Soul says *Soften for me. I am coming through*.

HOW DO YOU remain ever so humble when you are so revered? They asked the soul servant, who answered:

Everywhere I look, I see Holiness.

FOR WE WHO CHOOSE to be Lovers, who choose a path of divine beauty and genuine healing, our daily practice is to look upon all things through the pristine eyes of Sacred Love.

WATER CAN BRING down a mountain, carve a canyon grand, and raise up crops to feed millions. Water can bring your soul out onto your face in a sincerity of tears. It can bathe a molecule that becomes a village exhaling it into a warm matrimony of sky. Water is what Lovers offer each other through their passion. Water impregnates generations. Water revives what is wilted. Drowns what is destined. Reflects what is. You, dear soul, are water, too. Behold.

BELOVED, YOU CAN live your life as though it is a barren plain or a lush paradise. No matter how you choose, you will be proven true. Absence or abundance. Deprivation or decadence. You get to choose. May your vision and its offspring (your way of being) enrich this world. To begin, express your Love to someone whose heart needs watering. Help their drought become a divine deluge.

WEARINESS is a Love letter from your soul saying *Please. Let go of distraction. Remember me.*

Remember *you* tonight. Remember who you truly are. This is how you care for the world. For the world of your soul is the soul of the world. Bless you.

IF YOU CANNOT TREAT the land as sacred, you cannot treat yourself as sacred. For the soul of the land is the land of your soul. Relative, do you know what it means to be genuinely sovereign? It means you cannot own anything. And you cannot be owned. Indigenous ways.

WE ARE HEALING from the idea of ownership. Ownership of humans. Living things. Land. Sky. Water. Truth. Who clings to conquest ways shall perish. Who surrenders to earth ways shall be free. Please, accept this offering of soul water, sage, and sweetgrass for your journey home to Beautiful.

OUR BEST DAYS tend to happen when we fall into counting our blessings and not our grievances. Gratitude is a gravy that makes the meal that is every moment taste like the best thing you have ever been fed.

MY PEOPLE. We weave tapestries of our grief and glory just as homespun and normalized as grits and gravy, grain and ground. We drum sound. We get down. We kneel before the Profound. Glory sings to us in return.

WE FIND MOST CHALLENGING the realization that the world which needs most to change, the world we are most able to change, is the world inside us. We *are* world change, world illness, world healing. The beginning and end of the work is within us. The outer world is no more than what grows from the condition of every single soul.

We seek salvation through external transformation of others. But such transformation has no real roots if it is not a manifestation of deep personal healing and growth. Our ego wants to blame what is outside us for what ails us all. Our soul, however, recognizes it is a source of what lives outside us. In this way, nothing is outside us. All worldly ugliness and beauty have a kindred seed in the soil of our personal spirit.

These two transient weather systems birth one another continuously. Yes, we may touch the outer world. Our touch, though, is of a nature decided by our inner condition. Do not doubt that you can change the world. You have been changing the world since you entered it. Your implicit atmosphere of personal condition is your truest force for change. Touch that most of all.

HOW MANY HUMANS does it take to change the world? Just you. You just did. A single thought or feeling, memory or vision changes you. You are the world. When you change, the world is changed. Your power deserves a promotion. Name it your new leader.

YOUR INNER STORY is powerful medicine, dear soul. It can transform your chemistry, brain, body, behavior, heart, spirit, relations, and life. Shed the stories that do not serve your sacred freedom, which is a strand in the web of our collective freedom. Be a gardener in the fragrant fields of Love. Bliss and blessing flow out from you when you turn the soil of your beliefs and plant new seeds in your newly fertile ground.

Your beliefs calcified in you as a child, impressionable as you were to the hordes and herds rabid with fear. Now, you can choose your beliefs as your soul decides. Be that courageous. Dare to determine your own life. Roam the wilderness of your boundless possibilities. And when they call you to come back to the crowd and its vacant agreements, do not obey. Stay out with the plants and animals as they sing Creation's lush lyrics. Stay with living things. They who with each breath and heartbeat glisten with passion as they spark new verse.

IN YOUR DEEPEST PLACE inside, you just want to feel safe and Loved. Grant this to yourself. Grant it to the world.

How to coexist in a sacred way: Reciprocity. Mutuality. Symbiosis. Kindred giving. Go around the world offering your heart's own desire. See the world become more like the desire of your heart. Don't count what is returned to you. Don't count on anything. Your gifting is what blesses you. Give Love. Grant safety. Your needs are a divine instruction on how to live. If you want a guru, your heart is teaching. Every day. Free of charge. Follow the yearnings. Give up your learnings. Be a sacred student. Bless you. You are worthy of being Love.

BELOVED SOUL. What might your life look like if you realize you are a living prayer? How much permission would you give yourself to be free?

GRATITUDE IS NO small thing. It is the very perch upon which you and I manage, through all the chaos and pain, to stay in the world. More than that. It is the soul fire that keeps us desiring to stay in the world. Gratitude is how we hold onto life. I am grateful for you.

IF YOU BREATHE deeply right now, with your whole body, you signal your entire being to relax and release. Some might call this an act of Love. Go ahead. Be a Lover.

DROUGHT PREVENTION. Retain your own rain. Dear soul, you would be amazed at how powerful your own voice is when directed inward as a ceremony of praise. And how impressionable your soul is to your own sacred voice. As though they were made for each other. Because they are. Speak life into your life, and you may find yourself intimately acquainted with a consistent river called *Peace*.

I AM GOING TO tell you now that I Love you. If such rain has not often fallen on your hard, cracked ground, the words may hurt. The water may not soak in. But, you priceless treasure, I am going to tell you I Love you. One day, the rain may soften you. You will soak up the words and become a fertile bed from which Love blooms and blooms and blooms.

HOW YOU ARE with yourself is an announcement to the world. A declaration of intrinsic worth and value. A statement of expectation. A blueprint you wave before you. Others come to know your preciousness as they behold you being precious with you. You imprint your relationships with a code of self-regard. Consistency creates your aura of Glory and Grace.

SHE WAS DONE shrinking, hiding, bending, contorting herself to fit into a mold. She shattered the mold and expanded into her true form: magnificence. She lived as a mighty mountain. Her ministry was to be an uncloaked miracle free of shame.

SOME SAY PEACE is a magical happening you seek. What if, dear soul, peace is a flower you grow? And if you knew this, would you spend life seeking or growing? May you grow, and thus know, peace. All the inner gardening you do, every moment and grain of it, is a sacred practice. Practice. The word suggests repetition and patience. Like all flowers, peace has its seasons. Its dormancy, bud, and bloom.

Bless your peace flower with soul water, soul light, and soul soil. It just may propagate into a meadow of everlasting serenity whose fragrance and beauty enchant you even through difficult places along your way. *Peace be with you*, is not only a wish or prayer. It is also a truth. Peace be. Always. With you. As Love's divine breath. As life within you forever waiting to be touched by you. Into the sweet succulence of bloom.

BEAUTIFUL SOUL. This day you are given is not only for completing tasks. That is not the point of this miracle. This day is for you to inscribe the poetry of your soul on the living pages of this world. Today is for passion. The holy breath of a living life. If you can slow and feel, truly feel, the miracle that is this day you have been granted, the sensation can wash away your worries and revive in you a feeling, however fluttering, you might call Peace.

IF YOU TOUCH my soul ever so slightly, it may burst. I am a drop of mist resting on the flower petal that is this world. I am that delicate. Not as a weakness. As the power of tenderness. Which, after all, births all things. I have come not for harshness but for the bravery of gentleness. For the spice of sensitivity that gives flavor to life. For the compassionate nature of womb, and the merciful Love contractions that midwife existence through the Spirit door. I am a drop of mist. Made to burst. Nothing more.

WE ALL MOVE through this world interpreting others and ourselves through opaque windows of imagination, projection, defense, attraction, fear, trauma, prejudice, and assumption. What wellness we possess becomes the clear window through which we see others for who they are, and ourselves for who we are.

These wellness windows allow us to be a *seer of souls.* They tell us true stories. About others and ourselves. Painful true stories. Pleasant full stories. Being able to see clearly and interpret accurately are hallmarks of a healthy, beautiful life. Devotedly cleaning our windows of perception is the daily labor of how we care for ourselves and others. If you want a life of harmony, healing, and goodness flowing, take the soap and water of soul and compassion to the windows of your life.

EVEN IF THERE BE but a seed of healing within you, that seed contains a forest of abundance. A world of beauty. A universe of Grace. Have hope.

BELOVED SOUL. Forgetting who you are is a doorway to remembering who you are. When you see this doorway, step through it. You will know yourself in a way you have not before. This is the blessing of sweet reunion. Your whole life can be a tender tide of drifting away from your truth and finding your way back. No punishing yourself. Just recognition and Loving return. Welcome home.

DO NOT LET THEM SHRINK the glory of your name into their stunted, colonizing cage of soullessness. Your name carries oxygenating oceans of ages and ancestors and all their harvest of living. Do not surrender your name to the impotent plantation of truncation, nicknaming, bleaching, erasure. Resist the gentrifying onslaught of the false sand dunes of conformity. The letters and syllables of your name are a rebel encampment where your people gather. Do not let that fertile land be deforested, desecrated.

The integrity of your soul lives in the soil that is the sound of your name. Your spirit lives in your name. Your true name is mantra, medicine, prayer. It heals you and yours with its utterance. It is resistance song against the madness. Your true name keeps you from being swallowed by the sickness of supremacy.

Oh, you sweet tenderness. Confess. Confess your true names. Which may not be what you were given or what was plastered over your brilliance. Your true names may have been kidnapped, stolen away. Still, they call to you through the salt of your tears. If you do not know your true names, then this unknowing is a blessed doorway to a ceremony that will save your life. Step through.

Regurgitate the bland names through which they siphon your power. Season your life, not just your food. Season your days with your sacred names. Burn those false names. Awaken the wildfire in you. Save your roots. Save your soul. Save your freedom. Save your names.

GENTLE. The way subtle forest spring moves up through earth, blooms out through the soil surface, and pours its heaven over ground and glory. Gentle.

In the way you shed your many skins of seasons, releasing what no longer serves you, releasing what you see is not your essence. Gentle.

The way you hold ceremony and let those artifacts of your pain and past retire to the spirit pasture of other worlds. Gentle.

The way you breathe this day, forgiving yourself as you inhale the offerings of sky. Releasing your bondage of tension and trouble in the ritual of your exhale. Gentle.

The way you touch yourself. Caressing and Loving your tender lands and breezes. Gentle. The song you sing. A native flute, like sparrow, soft, quilted arrow of praise and worship. Gentle.

How you drop your tears like turquoise seeds to bless and birth jungles of life in plains of desolation. Gentle.

The way you remember. Everything. Your memory not constructing jagged edges for the ideas of what has been and what has been done to you. But shaping softness as you curate your collection of the shapeable past. Gentle.

The way you offer your Love in all its forms. Gentle. The way you gather Grace for all that every soul is and does and mistakes. Gentle. How you imagine your moments to come, be they daunting or delightful. The way you cradle and hush your fears. Gentle.

Your notions of the oceans of your Love and what those Great Waters are truly for. Gentle. The way you softly encounter living things. Touching a world of tenderness with the medicine of your tenderness. Gentle.

The silence you afford yourself. The bed of solitude in which you slumber for your repair. Gentle. The tides of your emotional art. The way you move your rivers through and set them free. Gentle.

Your language. Like the music of mystic meadows and dragonflies dancing, sunlight glistening through their wings. Gentle.

The kind Love letters you leave like endless leaves on countless trees. Prayers of peace sewn with the moan of the Love you make as you let your precious heart feel, and feel, and break. Gentle.

The way you gather yourself from the waving grass and sit on stones beneath shading trees and drink the soul of your life into the sanctuary of your Gentle.

TONIGHT. Let peace be your bed and blanket. Serenity your chaperone to sweet dreams. Deep breath. Release the angst. It may come back eventually, but you do not have to sleep with it tonight. Bless yourself with permission to relax and be at ease. Bless your tenderness. Grant your heart a deep retreat. Sweet dreams. Sweet soul.

THE PAINFUL THOUGHTS and feelings moving through you are echoes of stories planted long ago. The question is this: Is it more important to you to hold onto those stories, or to let them go so you may heal and have peace? You are in a relationship with each of your stories. It may be a good time to consider whether these relationships are good for you.

BEAUTIFUL, GLEAMING SOUL. You are the very first of your kind. Rejoice in the gift of your rarity.

A Loving word on caressing the tenderness of being you in a world that has never beheld a glory such as yours. Relish your relationship with singularity. It helps you participate in the human commonality with less insecurity and combat, and more clarity and Grace.

Even *you* are just now discovering you. Hopefully it will always be this way. The *you* of you is forever a soul surprise. An unlikely sunrise. Let sweet tears fill your eyes. Be in awe. Stay in wonder. Behold yourself. Hold yourself the way you would a treasure you just found. You just did. This very moment. Found a treasure. Now, open your unsure heart and practice the pleasure of being absolutely you.

THE WORLD HAS NEVER seen a *You* before. Don't hold back. Give them the full show. Your entire life is the sacred debut of you. This isn't an audition. It is the season of your audacity. You made the Big Show. Please feel free to show up as yourself. That. Is your medicine. For you. For all living things.

WHO ARE WE to reject the inspiration pouring through us? It is not the place of the musical instrument to refuse the song. Let through your sacred song. This is how you fulfill your life, become a good host to peace, and achieve being an ancestor who leaves wellness in your wake. Bless us. Bless you. Let Glory through.

YOUR PAIN IS YOUR origin story. Your legend lies ahead.

JOY AND PAIN may both be powerful wombs and doulas for change and growth. Choose the first when it offers itself. Cherish the second when it comes. Avoid dependence on either, for they are not meant to be permanent fixtures in your every moment. They are passageways. You are the passenger. Determine your sacred way.

IF YOU WANT SWEET dreams, put some sugar on your thoughts as you fall asleep. We do not dream to be shown our desires. We dream to desire what we are shown. May your night for you be holy. Your day a sacredness. Peace is your sacred poetry. Write a soulful verse today.

DEAR SOUL. Peace be with you. You are worthy of such. Regardless of the circumstances of your life, may you have the divine mercy and grace of peace. And, as you continue growing your idea of you, may you include peace as native to your soul. Drink sweet, wholesome, organic *identi-tea*. Bless you. Sending Love.

YOU ARE NOT your experiences. You are the soul water your experiences flavor. Vital difference. Flavoring can always be changed, evolved. And your soul water can always be purified. Downsize your idea of the power you believe your experiences have over you. Your soul water can ultimately dilute and wash away any flavor. You are that big. That bold. That blessed.

TOMORROW, YOU WILL try again. Please be ever easy on yourself today.

WORTHY SOUL. For your new sun journey ahead, add softener and use the gentle cycle. May you treat yourself at least as well as you treat your clothes.

I Love you. This is why I pour these medicine words. And may you remember: You are not on a journey home. You are home, on a journey. No need to live in a condition of anxious homelessness. You are already inside your perfect home: your sweet soul. Know this and live your moments to come at peace, dear one. Enduring peace.

BEAUTIFUL SOUL. When you feel overwhelmed, remember: You are not the ocean wave. You are the ocean, waving.

You are always larger, vaster, more powerful than the turbulence that comes and goes. The tides are in your nature, you sacred water. You were made to wave. And to be calm. Both are within you and at your service. Let them. Serve you. Here's to your soulful peace.

START A NEW FAMILY in your sweet soul. Raise a bunch of peaces. Let them go through adolescence and mature. Then set them free. Populate this world with the progeny of your own wellness and serenity.

MAYBE YOU ARE not just building a life. Maybe you are setting it free from all the lives that have imagined you.

THE STORIES WE tell ourselves about poverty and wealth rule the world. Through these fables we create gods out of monsters and demons out of saints.

WHEN OLD PAIN, no matter its origins or validity, erupts into the social theater, no matter its context or face, one thing holds true: Pathology has revealed itself, naked and raw and begging to be put out of its misery.

Cue the mercy of suffering, that desperate flame reaching for the sky to be doused. A haunted spirit more vulnerable than ever, for it has crawled out of hiding and is exposed and dilated for the soulful blade that will end its terrible life.

At some point, upon that late ledge and precipice of fate, a sickened soul must acknowledge its sickness or perish. So, too, a nation. Grace lives even in this truth. Behold the fury of a collective spirit terrified it will no longer be free to oppress the world. Behold Pharaoh, shocked and shrieking, naked and shivering in the moonlight of birth.

I WAS CUDDLING the moon last night. She told me the secret to her soul: She does not make the ocean dance. She dances inside the ocean. She dances so freely, so wonderfully that the ocean cannot help but dance, too.

YOUR DEAR HEART is not a landfill. Leave your trash elsewhere. Remove the litter. Let your heart be a garden park so pristine it draws the doves of beauty.

YOU DO NOT HAVE to hold onto your beliefs to hold onto Truth. If you remain open like a spring flower, Truth returns to you over and over, a Love-struck butterfly crazed for your nectar.

YOU DO NOT HAVE to prove yourself today. Today you can just be alive and grateful and growing. This is enough.

Accepting this is a vital root of peace. Bless you. You are worthy and precious. May you feel the flicker of a newborn peace. The flock will not leave you behind if you abandon anxious scrambling. But beauty will flock into your life if you learn to weave peace with the strands of your breath, body, and being.

You are not auditioning for life. You are already here. Release. Relax. Practice these simple repetitions. Watch your life grow fruitful. I send Love to wake your serenity.

MAY YOUR WONDROUS heart and spirit imitate sky today. Wide-open, unencumbered, and light as air. May the womb of life wrap its sacred self around you, a ceremonial blanket of care and assurance. May you be birthed into the bright light of your purpose and calling. May your giftedness spill out into the world, a treasure for all living things. May you suckle from the milk of true, everlasting peace, and sing a song that speaks your splendid soul.

QUERIDA. Tu corazón y tu alma son poesía. Tus ojos son poesía. Tus pensamientos y sueños y alegría y dolor son poesía. Tu aliento y cuerpo y ser, todo es poesía. Tu tierno verso reescribe el mundo en belleza. Que tu lírica cante para siempre.

Dear One. Your heart and soul are poetry. Your eyes are poetry. Your thoughts and dreams and joy and pain are poetry. Your breath and body and being, all poetry. Your tender verse rewrites the world in beauty. May your lyric sing forever.

SLEEP. You are a tranquil lake. Mist of your worries is lifting from you, evaporating into sky. Your heart feels lighter. Sleep seeps into you, a mystic wonder. A blissful current loosening your being. Liberating your bliss.

Your chest, your head, and neck, every part of you is drowsy, drifting, already dreaming. Your muscles loosen all over. A great migration of dreaminess moves through your land. Your body is becoming the ease of air.

Your molecules are slow dancing now. Your cells bathe in a Jacuzzi of calm, calm, calm. A gentle breeze gathers all your stories and will care for them through your sleep.

Sun sets in your brain and bones, caressing you along the fragranced path into peace. Peace... a light, easy music serenading you to let go of the day, of the season, of everything.

Forgiveness flutters in your heart. Takes flight. Takes so much tightness away from you. Leaves you bouquets of serenity.

A music moves over your skin, massaging your muscles, unraveling knots and thoughts. You are a tranquil lake sighing yourself to sleep. You are becoming night. Becoming restfulness.

Everything you are is healing now. Unspooling. Settling like leaves on your tranquil lake. Clouds lightly stroke your innerness as they move through. Your soul sips more peace. Joy is smiling inside you. Your spirit is such a tender, gentle breathing now. Free, open, easy.

Memories of your deepest peace, your most beautiful moments, all your glory, spread out through your mind into the valleys and plains of your body. Returning euphoria to you in visions. You are a great bamboo forest waving so slightly in the perfect breeze. Sleep.

You are the perfect breeze. The perfect breath. Sleep. Your name is sleep. Your identity is sleep. Your heritage and culture are sleep. You have made peace with sleep. Made it your safe space. Your sanctuary. Your oasis so cool in the heat.

Your nature is to sleep. You release into your nature. You surrender into your sacred medicine. Thoughts slow, grow silent, go to sleep. Sleep is rocking you rhythmically in its Loving arms. Swaying you just the way you like. Your nerves sigh sweetly. Stillness grows in your soul, a softness that makes you weep. You are soul and sleep. Soul and sleep. Soul and sleep.

THE MOMENT WE ACQUIRE any crumb of knowledge, we are vulnerable to corruption by the arrogance of delusion that we are knowledgeable. We sit in a small corner of an infinite library, read one book and believe we have read the entire library, assume we have interviewed the author, researched the entire lifetime of the author's inspiration and sources. We conclude that we must have built the library and curated each book.

We are inmates who read a hundred books while in prison and come out speaking as though we have gained all the tongues of Truth. We walk in nature, touch a leaf on a tree, experience epiphany, believe we know all to be known of nature, leaves, and trees. We experience one thing from one person from one social category and determine that we are the greatest authority on that category of humans.

We take classes and assume we have moved deeper into knowledge and not farther away from it. We offer our knowledge to others and if a single soul accepts it, we champion ourselves to have served the finest dish.

The very thought, *I know this*, ushers into our life the dying of our openness. With the words, *I know this*, we do not just close the windows of discovery, we shatter the windows and board them up with impregnable boulders of conviction. Convictions make us convict and yet we spend life fluttering into those flames.

You and I may often labor not to think ourselves superior to those who do not know what we know. Yet we do not even know what *we* do not know. And what we believe we *do* know is innately unknown to us, for we experience it through the distortion of our relentless prejudice.

In our trembling lifetimes, we live with knowledge the way a soul addicted to a thing lives with that thing. We crave knowledge and when we first taste a molecule of it, we loosen and expand to the blissful sensation of it pouring through us. So we consume more.

We grow euphoric and verbose, pestering everyone with our inebriation, naked of inhibition and frothing with pride. Soon the substance consumes us. We cannot live without it. We believe this knowledge-drug *is* us. Our identity is abandoned into a volcano of dependency.

This relationship bears children. One of its most powerful offspring is judgment. Judgment of others based on our new knowledge. Judgment of ourselves as enlightened. We fancy ourselves supreme. We reason we must be special if we are enlightened. And if we are special, and if knowledge has made us special, we have to acquire more of it.

We mortgage our health and relationships to get our daily fixes of exuding knowledge, of being the grand carrier of knowledge. These words are not doom. They are a path laid out before the healing spring water of humility. The hopeful moral of this story is that always our suffering is available to be released from us through a simple treatment: Say in your sweet soul, in words or wordless waves: *I do not know.*

YOU STILL EXIST. Even when you are not talking, listening, doing, going and returning, being seen. You still exist. Exhale. Release. You are not a living emergency. You are life. You exist.

IF YOU CULTIVATE QUIET. Caress your fears. Sugarcane your memories. Sweet talk your shame. Feed your relations. Fertilize your language. Affection your wounds. Harvest your dreams. Purge your false ideas. Remember your essence. Flavor your labor. Season your art. Spice your expression. Root your ways in ceremony. And wash your spirit clean. You can make a sanctuary of your soul.

Si cultivas silencio. Acaricia tus miedos. Endulsa tus recuerdos. Engatusa tu vergüenza. Alimienta tus relaciones. Fertiliza tu lenguaje. Encariña tus heridas. Cosecha tus sueños. Purga tus ideas falsas. Recuerda tu esencia. Sabore su trabajo. Sazóne tu arte. Condimente tu expresión. Arraiga tus caminos en ceremonia. Y lava tu espíritu limpio. Puedes hacer un santuario de tu alma.

A PEACE LIVES in your soul that is more than a rumor. Not a nocturnal rustle in the underbrush. Not a morning glint of sun. A peace lives in you, outrageous and obvious when you stop running from you. When you stop and open to the sufficient existence of your being.

Your peace is profound and pure. Already complete. It is the true vibration of your bones and blood, your breathing and billowing. Your peace is a broad, bright meadow within. An intrinsic songstress lake of rippling melody. Your peace sleeps beautifully. Wakes gently. Sees all things as Grace.

Your peace has its sovereign pace. It moves in its own rhythm. Swirls and dances and waves and wanders as it wishes. Your peace does not abide by your worries or busyness. Your peace does not ask. It is itself regardless of your permission.

Your peace is a river running underground, beneath your notice and lament. Your peace is spring water, filtered through ages of ancestral rock. Your peace keeps no clock.

Your peace is a passionate Lover, opening and opening to all living things. Showering its Grace on every ground. Filling your moments with its ministry. If only you would look, you would see your peace. If only you would feel, you would feel your peace. Your peace is with you, not away from you, not dormant, not dreaming. Wide awake and vital in its holy art.

For your remaining days and seasons, may you be awash in your own precious peace. All you have to do is believe in it. Open and claim it. Practice it. Let it saturate your life.

USE YOUR NOCTURNAL EYES. Night blooms bow at the doorway of dawn. Sweet breed of surrender. Bread of this briefest day. Brawn of this longest night. When the planets align, look into the night sky of your soul. Behold that convergence. What is more profound than you being born again today?

This new season on earth is a vast, aching womb. Pushing. Pulsing. Bleeding. Brave. Contracting. Expelling the foul flowers, inedible moss, and poisonous vapors of the past.

You sculpt beauty with the thoughts you choose. Your lips desire to speak a poetry of passion. Rumors of a great healing fall like petals on your skin. Your pleasure is in the purging. You soak in a hot spring named silence. Memories emerge from the mist. Of a time when we were in balance with Creation, our souls seeping humility, rooted in earth.

The salt of your weeping seasons the stew which feeds your quest. The vivid scent taking you now is the fresh communion of soil. You are a deep well in the desert. You are the cool water in the well. You are not the echoes of myth that have traced and taunted your life. You are a new story. Old origin song. You are the light of the fire and what dances in its heat. The universe is painting a masterpiece. You are the mortar and pestle turning the ochre and flower from pigment to paint, to poignant release.

ON EARTH WE SUFFER. What is left to us is to choose how we suffer. The pollen of suffering is pure. It holds no malice toward us. Wants only to be delivered to the next flower. Used. Transformed into a subsequent life. We can gather this pollen and concoct more pain. Or we can fertilize a miracle.

When we choose to suffer, we reject the idea that we are not helpless to suffering's tide. And yet, souls have proven that we can suffer with an abundance of Love, joy, beauty, and preciousness. We can move through this life inside an intentional parade of peace.

We have this choice not once a day, but in every moment. Beauty is an orchard in everything around us. Some move through, throwing stones at the fruit and cursing the trees. Some, though they suffer, can be seen with the juice of that plentiful succulence dripping from their mouth. They have discovered that life is a continuous offering. That suffering comes with the fabric of existence. And that how they tell this story in their mind, how they paint this grand mural of pain and pleasure, is the true Grace served for us beyond our understanding.

Behold the souls around you. See how they suffer. How they have taught you to suffer. Decide. Not only how you choose to live with this pollen's potential. But also how you will teach us the same.

SOME COME ACROSS the soul offerings you share and look for something to criticize, condemn, or demean. Their spirit is a vortex of unwellness that wants only to pull everything and everyone into that tortured pit. Others come across your Love offerings and choose to find whatever grains of beauty and medicine live in the serving. Please remember, dear one, you sacred artist, activist, healer, these souls are why you pour out your Grace.

SHE WOKE BENEATH a blanket of moonlight. Walking to the window she felt the moment seep into her, calling. She felt, at once, the touch of all her relations and the ardency of her divine aloneness. The window glass was cold. She touched it. Felt inside it yesterday's sun. *This would be the day.*

She caressed her body, all its land, and breathed with her every molecule, summoning peace. Outside now, the small fire she prepared was a bright jewelry against night sky. Its glow was rouge on her face as all her old shame-bred stories burned to ash and air. She had spent weeks writing them down. A ceremony she chose, to move beyond the pain and delusion.

The stories were gone now in mere seconds. Hard, generational calluses broke loose in her chest. It felt like old ice freeing itself from a glacier, to melt away. Tear-draped, she sat a long while beneath moon's matronage, acquainting herself with a new sensation of being. A waterfall of continuous release. *I will need a new idea of myself*, she thought. *And I will need to keep birthing myself. Forever.*

By the time sun began its spread into morning, she had new eyes. *Everything is medicine*. This would be her mantra. Her days ahead would still carry struggle. She smiled, knowing she would touch those struggles in a new way. She would live her life in a meadow of wildflowers, each a wondrous variety of kindness with herself.

SUPPOSE IT IS NOT TRUE that you are a prisoner to your past? Is it possible this rumor is untrue? What if you, in every moment, are the beginning of sunlight? The first leaf of spring. Come, walk this way out of the cloudy waters of your long dream captivity. You have this magnificent beach of gypsum brilliance all to yourself.

Some call this vision the future. You can call it your whisper. You need no longer drink from the rusted cup. The gleaming glass is brimming. Jasmine tea. Jade silence. Marry your peace before you marry anything. Sink into this hot springs of being, this adventure of moments. Strip naked and sigh inside the sauna of ceremony. Have words to feed your mind that heal it. Dilute your seriousness with silliness. Spill all the wine.

Wake sideways on a mountain you do not remember climbing. Stretch up into the blue and receive what the rare hawks bring you. Nap by a soft-spoken stream. Let the damselflies cool you with their diaphanous wings. Read all the romance stories bound up in bellies of the old trees. Write your own verses on the tall grass as your fingertips brush over.

Supply yourself joy. Kneel and gather it in a spirit of labor. Like fetching water at dawn. Bend low for the cotton. Free-pick it as a free soul. Yield your own harvest. Sew your own soul clothes. Meet the market with your makings. Give some away to those without coin. Learn not to admire souls wealthy on greed. Do not call them elite. Call the baker elite who shares bread with the stray animals. Call the blind girl elite who walks on one leg.

Go on a journey and take no steps. Travel far and do not leave. Go inside and open all your windows. Let breeze bring you its seeds. Consider your memories. Strain them like dry rice. Keep the ones that are true. Discover the false ones planted and pull them out by the root. Stain your eyes with beauty. See differently today. Weave wildly. Wander into the center of your soul and start a fire. Stay awhile. Stay even longer than that.

RHYTHM AND FLOW for you young ones... *Becoming Peace*. Peace. How many pieces of your soul does it take to get to peace? To get some real relief. To soothe the grief. To stop the thief that steals your lease on peace.

I'd say just a taste of peace is worth the pain of letting go of all the hurt and anger that chains you, that drowns you like a rageful rain. I'd say start with pain to get to peace. Stop running in circles trying to get away from the ghosts that haunt you. Break that lease.

I'd say stop and stand in the center of your life and look at it. Ask yourself *Who or what steals my peace?* The answer, precious soul, is always you. You steal your own peace. People can't steal what belongs to your soul. Peace isn't fruit on a tree somewhere for you to go and find. Peace grows on your inner vine.

Peace is not a thing you purchase, like fresh kicks or fresh rims or fresh houses in fresh hoods. Peace cannot be bought. But peace can be taught. Go find what feels peaceful and hang out with it. Listen to its story, its path to glory. Watch the way it moves, and thinks, and speaks, and acts, and heals. Imitate those peaceful things.

Notice what peaceful brings into your life when you give up the drugs of hate and hurt and harm and negativity. You build castles around your heart, thinking your cold walls will protect you, will kill anything that wants to kill you. But all your cold castles do is keep you from all the things in this life that can heal you. That can feel you. That can straight up reveal you.

And if you want peace in the world, if you want peace in your *barrio*, the place to start is not by casting stones at whoever roams too close to your homes, your hearts, your ideas of being safe. The place to start is the inner place, that place of grace, that sweetest taste, the video game you never play called *Soulfulness*.

The safest you will ever be in this *vida loca* is inside the peace you grow from spending time with you. Watching you grow new in every moment, every day, every thing that comes your way. Being brave enough to spill your tears, to spill them in creative ways, to speak your peace, and piece by piece to build your palace not of walls and hiding places, but of being real in this world, showing your true face, your true heart.

If you want to be a champion, do not run from what scares you. Enter what scares you and make it your friend. This is how you get the fear to end. You get in the ring and dance and sing and rhyme and write your verse. Rehearse. For becoming peace, you got to be humming peace and drumming peace and strumming peace.

Peace between souls and groups is a relationship that begins with the positive relation-flip between you and you. *That* is your lifetime crew. You want peace? Get jumped into that family that will never leave you, will always keep you safe and fed, not lost and cut and bled and left for dead.

Get jumped into being a peacemaker. Someone who can take all the pain and hurt and dirt and use it to build a life that shines, a life that rhymes, a life that makes your ancestors proud and lifts the little ones into a sun you never knew, so they can live the life they deserve.

You don't build peace from the outside in. You build peace by going home to you. That's how you begin. Pay attention to everything. Ask yourself *Is it full of peace or dying for peace*? If it is full of peace, then drink its peace. If it is dying for peace, then feed it peace. Even the most tortured soul can learn to be *peace-full*, can be a revolutionary for peace.

Never give up hope. Find your soul ceremonies that strengthen you, then do what the peaceful do. Live inside, and give inside, and work inside, and Love and heal inside, and inspire all the world inside your peace. *Peace*.

FROM UP HERE, you can taste the seasoning of beauty. See lowland and highland are the same land. Sky and earth each other's prayer. And if you can emulate the trees and their stillness. If you can breathe a bright retreat. If you can bargain the mountains to lend you their peace. Your soul again can fountain. Your sunrise once more released. Ease your precious river. Ascend the sacred breeze.

HOW TO START A WORK MEETING: From what prairie are your people? From the Tall Grass. How long have they lived there? Three thousand years. How old is your

people's pain? Older than the hills. Is it fertile? It has
birthed many medicines. What do you do after the rains?
We dance in the water.

Who gathers your people's tears? The children. Who
holds your people's stories? The old ones. What do you
create for trade? We weave sweetgrass. How do you stay
humble before other living things? We keep trying to
swallow the sky. Which is greater, a human, an animal,
or a plant grain? The glory that lives in each is the
greatest of all. What matters most, the outcome of our
work, or the spirit in which we work? Without spirit, our
work poisons all outcomes.

Thank you for sharing, dear relative. It is good to meet
your soul. Now, let us begin this sacred labor. May we
work in a good way. May our soul integrity never leave
us as we build this future together. May we stay on the
sacred path. May beauty live in the stories they tell of
what we do here now. May we earn the beauty they will
one day speak. May the truth of our offering live in the
wind and sing a good song, forever.

THEY WENT INTO PRISONS and lit poetry fires in the
hearts of imprisoned souls. The imprisoned souls found
their power and their medicine and broke out of prison.
The prison of their pain and the false stories they told to
keep their pain alive and growing.

Then the imprisoned souls ignited a revolution. They
began to speak new stories. Stories that resurrected
their soulfulness and demanded they be seen as human.
They went out into the world and realized that many
souls are imprisoned even outside of prison. They spoke
their freedom stories to those souls, too.

Soon, the revolution swept the broad land. Free souls everywhere, speaking and singing and dreaming and dancing and weaving and beading and drumming their stories. Gathering medicine and beauty and holding Love in ways that could not be broken. By anything.

HE SAT BY THE MOUTH of the sea cave. And wept and wept and wept. All the tears humans had told him not to cry came out. Soon, he could not distinguish his flood from the ocean waters. Something else happened, too. The tumors growing in his body transformed in that moment. Became pools of medicine.

In the days after, and for a lifetime, his body gradually healed from years of holding in his emotions. His mind and spirit healed as well. This felt so good, he adopted a new practice and grooved it deeply into his being. He practiced letting his tears run free.

He had been born a sky. Was hardened into a stone. Suffered as a volcano. Learned the ways of water. Became a living mist. His relations healed and improved. Generations after him inherited the fluidity of his earthly condition and his sweet practice of release.

TWO SEEDS BURIED in the soil were racing to be the first to sprout through the surface to be blessed by fresh air and sun. One seed gathered all the stories it had been told by the generations before it, and the other seeds around it. It believed in those stories without question. Those stories became its identity. The heaviness of its belief-slavery weighed it down, polluted its spirit, and blinded its seeing of its own true nature and beauty, and that of others. It never reached sky or sun.

The other seed, realizing that all stories are the breath of fear, or Love, or both, examined the very same stories accepted by the first seed. Upon examination, this second seed chose to release the false stories born of fear, and to be fed by the stories born of Love. This nourishment helped the seed realize it did not need to race to the surface. It only needed to discover and live out its true nature.

It relaxed. Opened its heart. Rose up in its own way and time. It broke through to the freedom of truth, and was blessed by sky and sun. It was so fertile, it birthed an entire forest. The seeds of which learned the wisdom of sifting their inherited stories, and the importance of bravely releasing the stories soaked in fear and delusion.

In the soil of your own soul, and in the soil of the world, within which you are a seed, are many stories. May you sift these stories. May you examine their roots, and wash them in the discerning waters of spirit and intuition. May you be brave enough to release what does not feed the collective wellness. Of which your life is both a seed and a story. Meant for sacredness.

REMEMBER AS A CHILD when you hid in the closet to taste the black mystery of darkness? Or the time you hid there to escape chaos and feel safe? Where are your closets now? Where do you retreat? Night is a closet, though you cannot sleep forever. The sun eventually comes. Sometimes your moods are a compass pointing you in the direction your soul yearns to travel. Pay attention to how you are feeling. Mine the meaning from your emotional meadow. Praise peace where you find it. Don't stop at being a peace worshipper or follower. Be a pastor. A preacher. Become the sacred words.

YOU FEEL SO MUCH shame at crying. Imagine if you were proud of your tears. How many of them would you set free, and how soft would your soul be from the watering? The heart pain you had yesterday resumed today when you woke. Water it. You will know when you quench its thirst.

I AM GOING TO TELL YOU a true story:

You overcome it all. The end.

The more you notice and celebrate even your smallest triumphs, the less consumed you are by your worries, fears, and challenges. One of the most powerful factors in healing is to recognize your healing. You, dear one, have overcome countless things in your lifetime. Reward yourself with moments of gratitude and peace. Meditate on your soul successes. Plant better stories. Harvest a better life.

DO NOT LET THEM bleach you. They will try to bleach your essence from your soul. They will try to bleach your name, your tongue, your truth, your culture. Stay all your wondrous colors. Paint this world in you. Your journey is not to become like everyone else. No one is like everyone else. Your journey is to live completely exposed to life and still retain the piquant qualities of your personal phenomenon. You are not here to satisfy. You are here to add a particular seasoning to our collective stew.

You marinated in the moments and marrow of your ancestors. You were ready at your first spark. When doubt and fear rise up in you, see them, greet them, invite them on their way. This is not when you turn and run. This is when you root and romance the soul of your soul. In your deepest dreams wakes a whisper: *I want to be myself*. Bring this whisper into your conscious life. Sing it as a song. Dance your wildest euphoria. If you can learn what you are, and celebrate it with the passion of birth, you will be free. And everything you set your eyes upon will blush afire with your soulful artistry.

FOR MANY REASONS, we take leaves of absence. Let us birth and cultivate a culture in which we take *leaves of presence*. Shifting our focus away from our absence from labor and onto our presence within ourselves, and our families and friendships. Our presence within our health and renewal and passions and birthings. Our presence within our grieving, healing, changing, and our new seasons of life. Send out the beautiful word: *I am taking a leave of presence. I will see you after I see me.*

THE BLANK CANVAS of this moment is yours to paint, dear soul. Regardless of your circumstance. You are the painter. The paint. The painting. Your life is art. Paint beautifully.

Our lives move from sorrow to song, from despair to joy, from fear to faith, when we move from seeing ourselves as consequence to seeing ourselves as creator. Ask anyone who has deeply healed: *When was the moment your life changed*? They will answer: *When I realized I could choose to heal*. Here's to the paint-ability of your life. And your giftedness to create a beautiful mural from the fine canvas of your soul.

THE SPREADING OF GLORY is not for the timid of heart, for the act is an art of abandon. It is for the brave dirt that dares become a garden. And for the carefree sky that dances everywhere it goes, in breeze and rain and rambunctious sun. It is for spiced souls such as you who add seasoning to every stew. Who lift the window blinds and let brightness touch everything to life. To life, to your spreading of life and Glory. Bravo for your endless banquet of joy and jubilation. Glory, Glory. Everywhere.

I SAT ON THE MOUNTAINTOP and thought of you. The breeze came to see me as I reflected on your journey and just how much you have endured. You tend to count your mistakes and shortfalls. I wish you would count your countless survivals. Your walking on coals to the other side of pain. Your many plantings of hope in the cold earth of despair. Your brave debates with fear. You are truly extraordinary. Because through it all, you persist in beauty.

SO MANY BEAUTIFUL ROSES growing in the soil of every living soul, every living thing. From my first breath I have been breathless. This Creation is a miracle that keeps me weeping. Glory sings to me. The Grace in my heart sings back. The two Lovers meet in the middle of every moment, and make a Love so divine, endless births come forth bringing more sacred music.

How can you not dance ecstatic to this jubilation? How can you not give away your heart to this endless sun and infinite moon? Even writing these words I fall in Love again. Its boundless lake will not release me. And so I stay. For a lifetime I stay. If you want to find me, be willing to lose your clothes and leap into this pure water. I have heard the impossible music. It has taken me. I am not here. I am everywhere the holy song makes its reverent home.

WHO ARE THEY to judge your sacred language? They do not know the beginning of the experience you are having, or the meaning of the paints you use to describe it. They are flightless birds criticizing the ones in the air for their technique. Let them come down from their lofty perch and grow their own wings. Then they will know what it means to experience the sacred sky.

AWE AND WONDER are apt medicines for life. With every breath, be breathless.

HOW MANY WAYS have you caressed your soul today? Keep going. This particular spa day happens only once in your life, and you, dear, are your soul's perfect masseuse.

SLOW THY ROLL. Rest is not death. It is life. It gives life. Births life. Revitalizes life. Preserves life. Heals life. Rest is life. I believe it was the ancient Egyptians, Ethiopians, Mesopotamians, or Mayans who first said *Slow thy roll.* Could have been Scooby-Doo. Or Pac. Anyhow, you may be afraid of what you will miss out on if you slow your roll.

It is true, you will miss out on many things: heart attack, stroke, loss of physical, emotional, spiritual and mental health, angst, anxiety, depression, stress, burnout, chronic fatigue, ill-fated decisions, poor discernment, emptiness, hollowness, wilted relationships, loss of inspiration and passion, Koyaanisqatsi (Hopi for *Life out of balance*), accelerated perception of life passing, depreciated meaning to your moments, whack creativity, increased anger, hostility, prejudice, bigotry, violence, sleep deprivation, brain damage, premature death, premature ejaculation, abbreviated orgasms, shallow intimacy, delayed onset joy, blindness to a million daily miracles, rejection of the infinite, incredible slow offerings of life. To name just a few. Fear not the slowing of the roll. Don't troll the slow roll. Slow. Thy. Roll.

MANY WHO CALL themselves mystics are as permeable as stone. Those whose presence makes you feel you are inside a mist between worlds, those are your mystics. Mist with them.

YOUR SKIN REMINDS them of the dark, unconquerable womb. In the rampage of their fear, you are Mother. Absolute beginning. Feverish and addicted to the illusion of control and conquest, they cannot fathom ever returning to the surrender demanded by the womb. So they seek to destroy the Mother they see in you. Even your aura is a womb. A tomb for those who fear freedom, theirs and yours. Life for those who taste the grits and greens and grief of your Glory and cry a never-ending Amen.

YOUR OWN LOVE heals you.

Pour inward, dear one. Pour inward. It is not that you lack Love. It is that your river needs to flow in both directions. What you are used to giving to others is a sacred water meant to nourish you first. Pouring inward purifies this water, filtering it through the fertile earth of your original spirit. Then when you share it, you are free to share without desperation, anxiety, motivation, or need. Love-water shared this way is a pure tonic for both souls. You can learn a new ceremony: soaking in the spring water of your own Love. Peace, healer. Peace.

WHAT THEY HAVE SAID about you is not true. Will never be true. The perceptions others have of you is at most a molecule of your entirety. More often, it is an aspect of a dream they have been living their whole life. A dream into which they have placed their imagination of you. Nothing you do can ever reveal to them your whole and accurate truth. Even you cannot grasp the all of you, for it is a mystic sacredness that wanders dimensions and stars, and has no end.

Practice letting go of worrying about how others cast you in their theater play. You are not here to act in their presumptuous production. Even if they Love you. You are not an image for them to project onto the screen of their storytelling. You are not owned by their idea of you. You are a free and sovereign sky.

All things in you are not beautiful. Yet you are in the beauty of all things. Recognize your glory. Ground yourself in the reality of it. Take a breath of your pristine air. Celebrate the miraculous union that is you.

YOU ONLY HAVE so much time left to let people feel how much you Love them. How much you care. You are holding entire stories in you of what they mean to you. You have so many ways to tell the story. Now is a good time to begin.

A PRICELESS CONVERSATION with your ancestors:

Thank you. Thank you for holding me all my life. I've been thinking about you. How was your childhood? What were the lands like that raised you? How did you come through your fears? What did you do with all that pain?

How did you prepare your favorite foods? Were you nocturnal or did you rise early, or both? How did you handle supremacists? Especially the ones in denial of their supremacy sickness? You know, the ones who thought they were the good ones. I would like to hear about your encounters with those.

Did you dream of the future? Did the past chase you through your nightmares? Was your world quieter than mine? How did you use the silence? Sometimes, I lean on you as though you were a giant tree in your lifetime. I hope that is okay. Please forgive the pain I have caused you. The pain I have caused in my life. It breaks my heart, yet I never arrive at perfection with that. I just don't want to be hurtful anymore. How did it feel to be free of enslavement? How did it feel to be your kind of slave? Thank you for keeping the land alive inside me. All these years. My heart feels you near, on my skin, in the air. A blanket you wove for me. Now I join you in the weaving.

FREEDOM IS A DEEP PRAYER for all living things. And the endless, hopeful labor to make it so.

JOY LIVES. It is not a rare artifact to be extracted from the arid earth of our days. It is not to be encased behind dulled glass in the cabinet and only taken down and dusted off in the finer moments. Joy is the heat cascading out from the flame of our faith that we can be joyful. We must tend to the fire of our faith. We must believe that joy lives in us without pause, through loss and pain and all conditions.

Yes, even during the foul breath of personal attack and in the wet tide pools of sorrow, joy is the very nature of our being. The spirit of life is joy, an eternal heat of wonder and expansion. When we disbelieve that we can be joyful, in any moment, we kill the flame that releases joy's thermal light. Joy can only be released through our self-permission to be joyful, through our courage to be joyful in the face of living.

Joy must be watered and sung to. It is a flower spirit, a purring persona that responds to our stroke. It is faithful, though it needs us to give it birth, grant it space. Open all the windows we keep closed in our minds. Joy needs us to douse it in the poetry of laughter, to braise it in smiles freed without public reason.

This world teaches many lessons. Vastly we have chosen the lesson that laments—the listing of all causes for shuttering joy inside the heart's pantry, sealing it from the light of choosing that would let its warmth come forth in ribbons. We have learned to witness life and yet not truly see its stream of reasons to be the joy that we are.

We spend lifetimes enacting funeral processions in the mind, in each mundane moment proclaiming: *Joy is dead*! We practice sad soliloquies for joy, enacting its burial repeatedly, throwing cold dirt of misperception over a corpse that is not there. Joy can never expire inside a living soul, though it can well be brought to sleep by our neglect.

Behold the bird that rarely flies, and only when all conditions are suitable. That bird is us. Our flight is joy and for this we have been given immutable wings. What *can* be mutated is our understanding that we possess wings for flight. What is divine within us waits to be celebrated even at the crack of wounding. For even clouds say something about the sun: its presence, absence, or many moods. Only by sunlight can we discern clouds as they traipse their forms and shadings across sky stage. Only by joy do we know the texture of our sorrow and thus find our way back home to peace.

Joy is that sun ready for us to let it illuminate our melancholy, to burn it away, or let it fall as healing rain. Joy is not a condition of our outer life. We need not scheme or search for it. The awesome breath of our conception made us joy, then we were born and quickly wrapped in many blankets of notion. We learned to gather those blankets for ourselves. Now we are swaddled too deeply in ideas of conditional joy. We have smothered the faith-fire of perpetual joy. It can be resuscitated.

All that is left before us in this recovery is to burn these many blankets, to relearn nakedness of being and all the roads of awareness leading back to the clearing where the burial stops and joy lives.

Joy Lives.

IF YOU WATER your soul with appreciation, affirmation, and celebration, you will not spend your life chasing other people's rain.

TEARS ARE HOW your soul washes itself. Let your sacred river flow. Take comfort. Beautiful things are being born for you. This is why it rains inside you. To soften the way. Cherish your river of feeling. It is carrying you to your ocean of peace, picking up sediment along the way that is the sacred meaning of your life.

EVERY MOMENT your body speaks to you: *Be kind to me. I am your earth.* Your heart sings: *Spark me. I am your fire.* Your soul whispers: *Fly in me. I am your sky.* And your tears tell you their secret: *Let us flow. We are your river to a beautiful life.*

YOU HAVE SUCCEEDED billions of times just to reach this moment. Remember. If you do not consider yourself a winner, maybe you do not recognize the evidence. Spend time in the garden of your identity. Appraise the resilience of your life. Sum your miracles. Fertilize your thoughts that say: *I am a phenomenal thing. And worthy. Black soil earthy. Down to my bones and marrow, I am worthy.*

ONE DAY, you will choose lasting peace over deep hurt. On that day, your precious life will be miraculously new. *I choose peace.* The beginning of the journey. Say the words.

WITHOUT LOVE, no compassion. Without compassion, no caring. Without caring, no truth. Without truth, no justice. Without justice, no healing. Without healing, no wellness. Without wellness, no freedom. Without freedom. No true life.

SO MANY SUNS in human form desperately seeking sunlight. Look within. Expand your personal sunlight. Bring your bright atmosphere wherever you go. Put hope in your heart pocket. Let beautiful thoughts board your brain train. Keep kindness close. Infuse your water with lemon and your spirit with joy. Illuminate your life. Sun bathe daily.

EVERY LIVING THING is Loving you. Why? You are a living thing. Awaken to the truth of the oneness of life. Life Loves itself. You are life. Unlearn the cultural untruth of separation. Begin today birthing your new identity: a strand in the web of life. Quivering with the energy of the web, which quivers with the energy of your strand.

Shed onto the ground your garment of loneliness and aloneness, and leave it there forever. Surrender into the union you have always been a part of and have run from. Like sliding into a warm bath, fall into this unconditional Love that is all things, that is you.

Finally know the peace of knowing Love. True Love. A sacred pouring from you, to you, through you. Feel this infinite grace. No more yearning. You are in Love's river. Love's river is in you. Home. Alive. Completely Loved. Spend the rest of your life feeling this miracle. Your actual life.

PEACE IS NOT something you go and get. Peace is an excavation. Unbury your peace.

Life's layers can bury your peace. Until you don't feel it in you at all. You go looking for it in the world, taking you further from your intrinsic peace. Breath by gentle breath, remember yourself. Bring up your peace from the sediment. Wash it in your tears of Love. Reacquaint yourself with your peaceful nature. Each time life's wind blows dirt over your peace, don't go looking outside yourself for your peace. It is with you all along. Turn inward and patiently bring up your peace. If you can learn this practice, you can hold your peace.

YOU MAY BELIEVE this moment is the bud, that one day you will enjoy the blossom. This moment is the fruit. Feast. Joy's fruit is always ripest right now. Don't wait. Don't miss the offering. Go ahead. Pluck and eat. Life is best when lived right now. The sweetness of this moment is gathered, waiting for you to bite in. Live this moment like an eager flower lives sunrise. When the next moment comes, live it that way, too.

OUR STRUGGLE is not between belonging and loneliness. It is between abandonment and freedom. Do not abandon your own soul. Stay. You will know freedom. Be what you want. Want what you are. If you want more music in your life, sing. More dance? Move your hips and surrender. More Love? Tap your heart-barrel and pour. You are the instrument of your own fulfillment. You could be bathing in peace right now. Stillness is the bathtub. Your Love, the water. Soak.

IF YOU COULD touch a thing with Loving kindness and have it change your whole life, would you? Good. Touch your heart.

LOOK AGAIN. This time with your true eyes. Your soul is beautiful. And you are worthy.

IT TOOK HER DECADES to truly, deeply fall in Love with herself. Perfect timing.

THIS TIME, instead of shedding only tears, she shed shame, sorrow, and silence. The old weight left her. Lightness arrived. In her heart, Mercy played new music.

HEALING OFFERS THIS amazing advantage: You can always start right now. No startup kit needed. No degree, guru, program, travel, book, or plan. Try a deeper, more Loving breath. A kind thought about yourself. Laughter. Tea with a friend. A parade of tears. Dancing to birdsong. Permitting yourself to say *No*, to not conform. Healing is not a quiz, there are no perfect answers. Healing is a potential living in every single moment of your life. Available and free. May you begin. Again and again. Forever. Welcome to your own personal Beauty Way.

HERE'S THE THING about fishing for compliments. What happens when there are no more fish? Affirm yourself in every moment.

FEEL LOVE FOR yourself daily so deep you cry tears of gratitude. Ache the miracle of you. Ache with awe and wonder. Grow emotional. Call forth your river to wash away the pain and sediment, and purify your soul. You have a profound journey to go on. Bring soul water.

EVERY SOUL YOU ENCOUNTER means the world to someone. Someone is trusting you to take great care with that one soul, in turn blessing the sacred web of life. And know this: Your care always circles back. To take care of you. We are relearning the oneness of life and sacred ways. Care is never individual. It is always collective. And yet always personal. When this is no longer a riddle to you, you will have bloomed into care's epiphany.

YOU COULD POUR yourself into caring for you and no one else. Then you would have one person caring for you. Or you could care for the world, including you, and have a whole world of souls more able to care for you. Practice spiritual math.

THOSE WHO DO NOT VALUE silence have not had the pleasure of experiencing soul-blessing silence. You have no precious idea what silence can offer until you let it take you all the way home. Some go to silence's front door, shuffle around for a moment, then leave. They say *I don't like silence. It's boring. It scares me. I feel anxious, lonely.* But these souls have not gone inside the always-open door. Have not exhaled and rested there, listened to the divine music. They do not know this kind of silence. Cannot grasp the luxuries inside its home.

BEING A LOVER has nothing to do with having a Lover.

Imagine if we didn't wait for special days, moments, or people to let Love fountain from our hearts? Imagine if we realized the revolutionary power of our own personal Love to heal, renew, and transform the collective heart of humanity?

In the ecosystem of true, sacred Love, no injustice can exist. No oppression, supremacy, caste, margin, or dehumanizing. Love is a fire that burns away all your illusions about what is real. Love's salve dissolves away your wounds. Even the wounds of your ancestors.

We keep waiting for a magical solution to our personal and worldly suffering. There is no magic for this. Only the unchanging truth and endowment of your essence: Love is your only way home to deep wellness and Peace. Wildly gift this fresh, unwilting bouquet today. Every day. Forever. No more portioning. Your Love is infinite. Share the whole feast.

YOU'VE BEEN THROUGH a lot. Hallelujah. Your moments make you. Give your whole life to healing and growing your power. So you can make your moments.

WANT YOURSELF more than anything in your life. You can always have you. Guaranteed. You having you is how you birth peace. You already have you. Accept the gift. You have guaranteed access to you. Open inward. Watch your outward reality beautify and multiply divinely.

HUG YOUR HEART tighter. Tighter than that. It has been through so much, and still dreams. Your heart is an underrated Lover. It takes a beating and keeps on caring continuously. Every heartbeat is a prayer, dream, hope, faithful optimism. Pour your tender Loving care there first, the center of your emotional life. If you can comfort, soothe, and reassure your heart, you can fortify and calm your life waters. That you may clearly see your true soul reflection and manifest in your life what your heart drum beats out to you.

FIND THE POETRY and grace in every fertile grain of your life. Harvest, share, feast, and plant again.

THEY WILL ASK why you spend so much time alone. And you will say *I am never alone. My soul is perfect company. And so is Love.*

IF YOU GROW QUIET enough, you just might hear your heart and soul saying *Let's Love and heal each other.* When your essence speaks, write down that mystic poetry. Give life to your life.

THE WORDS YOU THINK and feel and speak become the jewelry or junkyard of your soul. Purify. Words are living things. They must feed. Can be medicine if you choose them well.

SHE PRAYED and gave herself a new name: Peaceful. *Her soul listened and filled with everlasting peace.*

Often only our identity holds us back from a new, more beautiful life. Be willing to do the work of shedding your old, worn out ideas of yourself. You will shoo them away. They will keep coming back like persistent moths. Until you birth big, bodacious butterflies. New ideas of you. Now your butterflies leave no room for moths, and the new you takes flight, dripping with nectar like a nubile flower in bloom.

OFTEN, THE ANSWER IS... Do less. A lifetime of doing can bury you in doing. Doing is not always being. Doing can undo being. Being need not be done. If it feels to your tender heart and weary soul as though peace is often just beyond your grasp, may you try the art of doing less. Learn to trust in the fruitfulness of being. If you fall in Love with being, you will discover the joy and lightness of at last coming wonderfully undone.

I LOVED MYSELF DEARLY TODAY. It was enough.

I Loved myself dearly today. Over and over. Took myself up the mountain and cried. Let the wind, that mystic masseuse, have its way with me, moving over my skin like rivers of ancestors moving over the plains and prairies. And I cried. I heard the jingle dancers in the song of the petite birds. And I cried. My crow and hawk cousins circled over, calling out to me. I extended my arms as wings and Loved them back. And I cried.

I chose silence. Over and over. Its sermon pouring into me. I prayed to purify my life and heal this desecrated land that is my heart. Blue sky blanketed my shoulders. Bowing sun still a medallion of sacred beads on my chest. I chose to rest. Even in the midst of this shifting, a new tenderness. Beauty everywhere only Love can see. I saw it in waterfalls and streams and the mating of things. And I cried. I Loved myself dearly today. It was enough.

ONLY THROUGH THE HEART may we touch the soul. And this, forever, is why we are here.

Sólo a través del corazón podemos tocar el alma. Y esto, para siempre, es por lo que estamos aquí.

KINDNESS AND CARE for others grows kindness and care in the world that then arrives back to you. The garden outside you feeds the garden inside you. The reverse is also true. May you feed both gardens. Sending you Love. For you are always worthy.

SHE WAS RAISED to be hard on herself. So she spent her years growing gentle. Her whole life bloomed.

You can always be gentler to you. If you believe you cannot, this is the harsh conditioning of *doomfulness* speaking. Daily practice births miracles. You deserve and are worthy of ease. You inherited punishment spirit. Endow those who come after you with self-Love ways.

SHE USED TO PRAY for someone to Love her. Then she realized she was that someone. Her fear, once a roar, became a gentle whisper. She was finally free.

When you know you are Loved, and you know you are your own Lover, you know you are not alone. Fear dissolves like mist from the soul of your life, which is the life of your soul. May you Love yourself with a saturating shower. Right now. Feel your Love. It makes all things new.

WHEN THE PAIN becomes unbearable, over and over say *Thank you*. Gratitude is a medicine spirit. As you fill your heart and soul with gratitude, it acts as a painkiller, softening the sharp edges and hard ache of your hurt. It displaces pain with its Love tonic.

Say thank you for pain as a mysterious architect of your transformation. Thank you for being alive. Thank you for your breath, heartbeat, and body. Thank you for your every moment of being. Thank you for the approaching end of your pain, for a new season of healing and peace. Thank you for sky, earth, water, and sun. Thank you for kindness as it stays in the world. Thank you for all your relations.

Thank you for your endless miracles, your infinite journeys, your ceremony of being. Thank you for your sacred blanket and beadwork of blessings. Thank you for the song that comes from your soul, the yearning prayer that is your tender, triumphant heart. Over and over, breathe out, summon your relief mantra and say *Thank you*.

OPEN THE EYES of your soul and look at everything. Know you are looking at Sacredness. Love accordingly.

ALWAYS BE HEALING. We are continuously impacted by life. Like moons forever pockmarked by asteroids and meteors. It is never true that we have no need for healing. No matter how much healing we have done. No matter how well our life is flowing. Do not schedule healing like a vacation. Live in it as an atmosphere. Let healing become as constant as your breathing and your heartbeat. Rejoice in the ceremony. Become your soul's favorite masseuse.

YOUR EVERY THOUGHT can be poison or medicine. Can bring pain or paradise. Choose wisely.

HERE IS A COMPREHENSIVE list of things you should beat yourself up for:

YOU WILL KNOW the ones who garden their mind and heart daily. Beautiful thoughts, feelings, and ways pour from them. Drink from those fountains. Become one.

IT DOES NOT MATTER if they get you as long as you got you. Get your own back. Your life is a journey determined by you more than anyone else. Practice not harming yourself. Practice freeing yourself from fear and old unhelpful ways. Cultivate belief in yourself by believing in yourself. One moment at a time. Practice releasing your need for people to get you. This need is a prison. A recipe for hurt and a limited life. Those who get you are frosting on the cake. Your self-embrace is the cake. You ought to be the most jubilant person in the world about you. Be a connoisseur of you. You get you. Get it? Got it? Good.

CARS HAVE BUMPER stickers like: *Baby on board*. People should wear signs: *Healing in Progress*. For every soul you look upon, healing is in progress. Be gentle. Patient. Forgiving. Understanding. Your turn will come when you need the same.

IF A THOUGHT CAUSES you pain, practice not thinking it. If a thought causes you peace, practice thinking it. If an act causes you harm, practice not doing it. If an act causes you healing, practice doing it. If a feeling causes you suffering, practice releasing it. If a feeling causes you wellness, practice feeling it. If a person causes you hurt, practice forgiving them. If a person causes you joy, practice cherishing them.

If your kindness causes you happiness, practice kindness. If your unkindness causes you sadness, practice kindness. If Love causes you life, practice Loving. If beauty moves your soul, practice soulful beauty. If prayer brings you bliss, practice being a prayer. If being born causes you to be washed and new, practice birthing yourself in every moment. If living causes you to cry gratitude, practice being all the way alive.

LIST ALL THE REASONS you should be unkind to yourself. If you have listed anything, it is time to meet yourself again. As a Lover. Love your soul. Love it.

THE QUESTION WAS: Where do you live?

And she said: In my soul.

Homefulness. The anecdote to psychological, spiritual homelessness. A condition of being meaningfully present within yourself. To experience an enduring peace not dependent on external sources. To grace your own life with inner contentment. To grow comfortable spending time inside your own textured terrain, exploring your vast territory. Learning, healing, evolving in intimate communion with your divine being. Not existential crisis. Existential bliss.

Home, no matter where you are or are not. Home, no matter who you are with or without. Home, no matter what you are doing or not doing. Home, no matter how you are seen, regarded, imagined, presumed, judged, condemned. Home inside your soulful roam. Free of anxious wandering and pervasive fear. All up in your spirit garden. The practice goes like this: Breathe to inner stillness. Return to inner reunion. Observe and release old emotions and thought patterns. Birth and nurture new ones. Peace by peace, build your home.

PEOPLE WILL JUDGE, convict, condemn, and crucify you. You are in High company. Love regardless. Be Love. Sometimes especially those closest to you will convict you. They are projecting their inner nightmare onto your sweet soul dream. Love regardless. You see, you must be what you came here to be. You simply must. All living things are counting on you to be you. This is how we keep harmony and goodness in the world. By being true. Regardless. Bless you. And all your relations. All things are your relations.

EVERY MOMENT of your life you have the opportunity to complain and fill yourself with poison, or give thanks and fill yourself with paradise.

YOUR LIFE DOES NOT determine your ease, peace, and happiness. Your thoughts about your life do. Think beautifully. Beautiful days are born of beautiful ways. Beautiful ways behave how Beauty says. Whatever you are experiencing, Love yourself enough to translate all of it into beautiful purpose. Into sacred song. If you are going to persist in anything, persist in seeing, seeding, and sowing a beautiful life. Big hugs. Big Love. For all living things. For all our relations.

WHEN I LOOK INTO YOUR EYES, I see all your ancestors smiling. Be encouraged. You are truly wealthy. Creator. Creation. Created. All of this is in you. You are not alone.

You are not even really you. You are life looking out through a soul window at itself. The idea of you as a lone individual is a cultural creation from an unwell culture. You are all your relations. All living things. You are abundance. Fruitfulness. Plenitude. You are not impoverished. Not denied or lacking. You are treasure and treasured. Hope of sunrise. Reassurance of sky. Feel your wholeness and totality. Feel it and cry.

BELOVED, WORRY NOT ABOUT ACHIEVING. Learn to be. That will be your greatest achievement. Your existence is a miracle, a monument, a majesty all by itself. You cannot be more worthy than you were when your spirit joined this world of living things. Unburden yourself of feeling inferior, insufficient, incomplete, unaccomplished. Your soul is the accomplishment. Behold the masterpiece you are, always were, and always will be. Return from the endless wander of doing. Come home to being. A feast called Peace is waiting at the reunion place. Inside your soul.

IF YOUR HEART is tender today, may you feel all the Love that is Creation, holding you, singing you to comfort and peace. May sky, sun, water, wind, land all touch you with their affection and heal your heart anew.

YOU ARE LIFE looking out at itself through the window of your soul. That's how great and un-alone you are. Behold the beholding that is life unfolding through you. Find your peace in that miracle. It is one. You are one.

IF YOU ARE UNSURE which way to go, Love is always the way to go.

DIG DEEPER. Peace is not at your surface. It is in your soil (soul). If you climb a mountain hoping for it to bring you peace, you may reach the peak and find peace dancing on your face as breeze. You may also find that peace has not penetrated the depths of your heart. This is because peace does not arrive from outside you. It wakes from within you.

Peace is a seed inside buried beneath layers of how you have experienced life. Those layers consist of stories. Those stories are energy. As you release those long entrenched stories from your mind, spirit, heart, and body, you excavate and wake your peace. Your new energy, like sunrise, leaks out over everything. Now you are the mountain and its breeze. And others may seek you, seeking peace.

YOU WILL KNOW you have entered a new territory of the soul when you stop looking for reasons for being kind.

A TRUE LOVER does nothing at all. Love is an undoing.
Bless yourself. Come undone.

SOMEONE TOLD YOU that you were a piece of gold and
you blushed, thinking it a compliment. You are the entire
gold mine. Raise your value. Your valuation of yourself
determines your life far more than other people's
devaluation of you. Stay in touch with your divine origin
and nature. Remember, your worth and worthiness are
infinite. Don't just praise your value. Raise your value. In
the way you treat yourself. In the way you treat others.
In the way you treat your life. Plant beautiful seeds. Raise
them. All your relations will reap the harvest.

YOU CAN ALWAYS be a little kinder. In this world, we are
all afraid and vulnerable.

IT IS TRUE, you can do many things. But can you do
nothing? That may be the greatest doing of all. Rest.
Breathe. Be still inside. Let your spirit graze on ease. You
keep tying knots in your soul. If you let go of the rope, life
unravels the knots and the knots go back home to peace.

IF YOU LOOK FORWARD to your joy, you will always be chasing it. If you look inward to your joy, it will always be waiting for you.

BEAUTIFUL SOUL. Kindness is the medicine you have been seeking. For everything. Broken hearted? Be kind with your thoughts and feelings. Kind with your memories and birth into new season and life. Ailing in your body? Be kind with the food you eat and in your movement, rest, and activity. Exhausted? Be kind through sleep, retreat, and renewal. Patience is deeply kind.

Conflicted relationships? Listen compassionately. To both tender souls (you and the other) beneath the surface. This too is kindness. Carrying anger and resentment? Be kind and forgive yourself. Be kinder yet and forgive them. Feeling lost and stuck? Courage is a kindness. Dare to risk, change, and grow. Feeling stress and anxiety? Breathing deeply is a great kindness. As is releasing worry and burden. Doubtful and fearful? Faith and belief are truly kind. Swollen with all that you suppress? Tears are a kindness gift. Laughing and howling, too.

Being true to yourself is kind. Try not conforming. Care about lives not your own. Such kindness returns to you endlessly. Justice is a fierce kindness that spreads like fire. Light that match. Love the human flowers people call weeds. This is divine kindness. Your soul wanders this world looking for safe places to land. Give it kindness. Let it carry that grace everywhere it wanders. Soon, it will not want to wander at all.

INTERRUPT YOUR REGULARLY scheduled broadcast of negative self-talk with an Aura Alert: I AM INFINITE LOVE. If you are infinite, you are unconditional. If you are unconditional, the conditions of your life do not determine your essence or hope. Your essence is *hope-full*. You are not dependent on Love or good times. Good news: You are Love. You are the good times. Drop your heavy clothes of identity. Your soul is a nudist and wants to shine.

BEAUTIFUL SOUL. All that you seek in the world exists inside you, in purer form. The answer to your suffering is not to fill your emptiness with trinkets. It is to recognize your emptiness is a paradise. Taste that garden. Know peace.

WHAT WE TOUCH with Love grows more Love-like. This is our transformative power. We own the sublime gift of touching, a gift that heals the world.

JOY ASKS YOUR HEART *Shall we dance?*

Speaking for your heart, you decline, saying *We are waiting for a good reason to dance.*

Joy asks *A reason such as?*

You say *We should be happy before we dance.*

Joy, perplexed, moves on to a more willing dancer.

SOME PRACTICE JOY. Some practice misery. Be careful whose class you sign up for. Choose your teachers wisely.

JUST BECAUSE THEY HAVE A NICE body, face, hair, bank account, home, family structure, job, or social stature does not mean they are kind to themselves, or are free of pain, or have peace. Do not envy or idolize. Open your caring heart. The most destructive disease of our time is human judgment. We have heart work to do.

BEAUTIFUL SOUL. Are you done promoting your pain? Hopefully you have realized its ambitious ways. It wants to be hired for every position in your soul venture. How about lending your joy a hand? It could use an advocate. It won't promote itself. But if you sing its praises, it will do its job and change the culture of your entire life.

PLANT A LOVING THOUGHT about yourself deep in your soul. Water, sun, slow sing. Repeat. Harvest your beautiful life. Plant another one. And another one. Peace isn't a gift that arrives. It is a seed you plant. Over and over. Soon, your own sacred forest of serenity.

LOVE SPEAKS INFINITE languages. In your lifetime, learn them all. Love fluency will save your life. It will heal your most profound wounds. Bind up your sorrows. Cause you to spill medicine where you go. Wilted flowers will revive to your divine dialect. The world itself will be solved inside your soul. Have only one ambition: Be Love's greatest interpreter, ambassador, connoisseur. Pour that eternal wine.

AN UNDISCOVERED paradise lives in you. Feel something true. Open that door. Go. We cannot measure the glory that grants us peace. May you know, dear one, the fragrance of your true soul. May it intoxicate you into a life of Love. Which is of course a Love of life. May your beliefs dissolve into Love. May your ways dissolve into Love. May your encounters dissolve into Love. May your aura become a pleasant place to live inside, a safe spirit to walk beside, a song so soulful it serenades sun and shadow and sends them both to serenity.

TONIGHT, BEHAVE LIKE the moon. Glow over everything. Be still. Hand out peace. Inspire awe. Embarrass the stars. Wake the poets. Dance the tides to life.

BEAUTY REGIMEN: All day, every day, write Love letters with your heart to every soul. Include yourself on the list.

HEARTBREAK is the nightfall just before the next sunrise of your sweet soul.

SHAME IS A BULLY. Weak once you stand your ground. Back it down with inner praise that soaks your bones and fills your heart with your native music. Shame cannot live inside a heart consumed with cherishing itself.

YOUR THOUGHTS WILL BE okay without you. Rest.

Send your thoughts out to go play. Sometimes, Loving yourself looks like nothing at all. Restfulness is a foundation for an active, creative life. Even Day itself rests. It is called *Night*.

You can teach your mind to calm its frantic thinking. It can become a tranquil lake. Whatever you struggle with becomes more manageable with stillness and rest. Everything you need healed is waiting for your blessing. That blessing is rest. Rest signals your healing things to commence. You think your thoughts need you to constantly shepherd them, or your life will fall apart. Often, your thoughts just want to dream and graze on their own, and for you to leave them at peace.

Go drink tea or wander a hillside. When you return, your thoughts will still be there. And your life, instead of falling apart, may just finally come together. For you are a rechargeable thing, designed to be at your best when you truly rest. Now, go get blessed.

SOLITUDE WILL NEVER leave you alone. Solitude is not the same as aloneness. Aloneness is a vortex of despair. Solitude is a sacred sun dance. Aloneness is a spiritual, psychological, emotional quality of inner homelessness. A painful sense of disconnect, an anxious alarm, a sensation of jeopardy. Aloneness says *I have nobody. Nobody notices me. Nobody cares. I am apart from all things, so I should suffer.* And so you suffer.

Solitude is a state of abundant companionship with yourself and with all things. Solitude is a calming union. A stillness returning you to your truer expansive you, activating and recharging your life force in unique ways.

Solitude manifests great lakes of peace in you. Looking into those diaphanous waters, you see the face of clarity looking back. You renew your vows of sacred living.

In this modern life, we suffer from so many voices forever in our head. Our brain and nervous system are fried. Our spirit is spent. Our human mind goes insane without sleep and silence. For silence, grant yourself the jubilation we know as solitude. Learn its life-restoring ways.

YOUR THOUGHTS are not your soul. Your thoughts should be your acquaintance. Your soul should be your Lover.

FREEDOM ASKS only one thing from us: Pass it around.

WHEN YOU SPEAK in the dialect of Love, you speak for Divine Sacredness. Every other expression is blasphemy.

THIS FACE. This face like the moon tonight. A warm, round tortilla of light. Glowing sky candle. Earth smiles at this face. Trees and deer smile at this face. This face is a land of song. A territory of rivers. This face holds meadows and breeze. Holds stories of pure Love. Secrets of children. Fragrance of jasmine and rose. This face is the moon's full body, naked in light, which takes my breath away. This face.

Esta cara. Esta cara como la luna esta noche. Una tortilla cálida y redonda de luz. Vela de cielo brillante. La Tierra sonríe a esta cara. Los árboles y los ciervos sonríen a esta cara. Esta cara es una tierra de canciones. Un territorio de ríos. Esta cara contiene prados y brisa. Sostiene historias de Amor puro. Secretos de niños. Fragancia de jazmín y rosa. Esta cara es el cuerpo completo de la luna, desnuda en la luz, que me quita el aliento. Esta cara.

WHAT PLANET are you from?
Love.

Why are you here?
Love.

What will you die for?
Love.

What is your language?
Love.

What is your secret?
Love.

Your favorite scent?
Love.

Your favorite intoxicant?
Love.

What do your prayers sound like?
Love.

What is your soul made of?
Love. Love. Love.

PLEASE DO NOT confuse the popularity contest for the worthiness of your soul and what it needs to thrive. You were worthy at conception. You are an organic beauty and greatness who needs no additives. Show up as you. No masks, costumes, or performances needed. You are always enough. More than that. You are always priceless. Don't sell your soul. Comprendes? Bueno.

DO YOU SCAN yourself looking for flaws? Scan your life looking for soul. Be a soul digger. You will find what you seek. And what you find will wake your Love. For you.

SOMETIMES, NOT FREAKING OUT is self-Love, too.

Panic. Despair. Stress. Anxiety. When we let ourselves fall into a story that we are in crisis, we flood our entire being with abusive chemicals that do real damage. To us and the world. Freaking out is a ceremony we perform at the end of a habitual story of doom. Learning to stay centered in a story of, *I'm okay. It will be okay,* even in the midst of real crisis, is a learned act of self-care that blesses you and everyone exposed to you.

Exposure. What are we contagious with? Because everyone is catching something from everyone. Catch peace. Practice peace. Exude peace. Your new name is *Peaceful.* May you grow used to answering when your true name is called.

FEAR AND ANXIETY often say *More, more, more.* Soul often says *Less, less, less.* Soul knows best. Soul is a savant that offers lessons for free. Enroll. Attend class. Practice. Graduate. Enroll again.

YOU MAY OBSERVE the evolution of the soul through the singing of these four lyrics:

I want, I want, I want.

I have, I have, I have.

I am, I am, I am.

All of this is Grace.

YOU ARE KEEPING a fire in the wilderness. It is cold and dark, so everyone wants to come near the fire to be warmed and have their life illuminated. Out of Love and compassion, you want them to be fed that, too. But if you keep focusing on gathering more people to the fire and keeping them at the fire as long as they need or want, eventually the fire will die.

You are the only one able to keep this fire, for it is your soul fire. You have to consistently tend your fire so that it may remain a source of warmth, light, comfort, and safety. A fire needs fuel and air. You are the one to provide those things in an essential way. Other fires are communal and other people may join in tending them. Your soul fire fundamentally depends on you, even if others can provide offerings. May you keep your fire bright.

BELOVED, WHEN MOON bows tonight, her alabaster face aglow and blushing the tenderest Love, her robe illuminating the whole sky, make sure you are ready to be filled with all she offers. Make sure you are dissolved and open, an ocean of tears and trembling. She shall not grant you this particular Love light again.

EVERY ONE OF US has been taught anxiety, whether or not we realize it. Of course, life can create a natural stress response. But the chronic overstaying of anxiety is very much a social conditioning, a sociobiological inheritance. What seems like it *just appeared* often was there all along, primed and waiting, often even rooted in the genetic artifact of our ancestral anxiety and trauma.

Perhaps most important is that we can unlearn anxiety and learn more empowering responses to and associations with life. With determination, devotion, patience, and practice, we can manifest a manner and mindset of calmness. Identifying the root of our anxious responses is a start. The journey beyond that is a matter of faithful investment. Science is learning what ancient Indigenous cultures have always known: Our perception and inner narrative create our truth, which then shapes our life.

SHE LEARNED to honor all she was instead of criticizing it. Pain eased. Peace came.

Self-criticism is a generational infection we catch from others. Love is the ointment, purifier, vaccination, and immune system. As you swim upstream against a cultural current that degrades you, may you take long baths in the natural hot springs of honoring your sacredness.

I am a sacred thing. Say it until the embers catch and flame in you. Forever.

YOU DO NOT NEED TO keep up. You need to slow down. We all need to slow down. Do not believe the hype of an unwell culture. Anxious rushing and doing only breaks you down, hurting your people. It feeds a greed-and-oppression-society and the gatekeepers who control it.

Instead, imagine the higher wealth of your wellness. Imagine it all day long. Every day. One of your most Loving acts is to slow down and be gentle with the flow of your life. Slowing down lets your whole being take a breath. Contemplation replaces busyness, creating clarity and tranquility. Your decision-making becomes more intuitive and fruitful. The energy you touch others with feels better to them, influencing their own stillness. Your life will be and feel richer.

You don't have to keep up with a nervous herd racing over a towering cliff-side. Slow down and you will have your abundant valley. The first flower to arrive will be peace.

YOU ARE NOT A SAND CASTLE at the mercy of the ocean. You are the moon that inspires ocean-dance. Do you tell yourself fables and myths about the sky falling on you and other impending disasters? You can change your inner condition to peace by changing your inner stories to power. Start with this legend:

The soul I am is untouchable, unconquerable, and all-capable. I am safe. I am sacred. I am forever free.

You are a glowing thing. You will always sway the tides. Affirm yourself like your life depends on it. For it does.

AUTHOR YOUR OWN healing. Literally. Create the story. Maybe you have so much trouble feeling Love for yourself because you see yourself through a lifetime of other people's stories about you. Put your worth and beauty into every inner story you tell for the rest of your life. Describe your healing even before you heal. Author your own healing. Own the words. Plant the seeds. Raise the crops. Harvest the bounty. Let all your generations feast.

WANT A NEW tattoo? Ink your soul with peace.

GRANT YOURSELF REST, dear one. Reject the oppressive social pressure to grind until you lose your mind, your health, your life. Uproot the cultural guilt in you that says you have to be doing something. It is killing us. Choose life. All living things rest. Be a living thing. We need your singular soul not doing, just being.

If you can learn to be at peace with your existence itself, nothing added, you can taste freedom, wellness, and purpose at their peak. After a lifetime of adrenaline state, your system needs to be reacquainted with what it feels like to be restful. Practice patiently, not as yet another adrenaline-soaked task. Keep bringing yourself back to letting go.

So many modern remedies for our exhaustion. One glaring, ancient, proven medicine: May you bless your tenderness, your stress, and your heaviness with rest. Sweet, old-fashioned rest.

SOMETIMES, WE TREAT our feelings as assignments. As though we need to do something grand with them. Sometimes, all we need do with our feelings is feel them. What do we do with breeze? We feel it. Cherish it. Let it move through. Our feelings are a kind of breeze. Feel me? I feel with you.

YOU DO NOT OWE ANYONE your exhaustion. Please stop treating yourself this way. Deep rest begins with permission: *I have the intrinsic right and sacred need to rest.* Mantra these words.

Many of us do not know what it feels like to be truly rested. A modern tragedy. You can be a whole new person. You can have a whole new life. Practice noticing your sense of obligation to busyness regardless of how you are feeling. Practice releasing this idea. Sacrificing yourself to exhaustion does not make you a good person. Your goodness has nothing to do with exhaustion.

Do not segregate your rest. Let it flower all through your day. Even in the way you breathe. Quilt it into your active moments. Weave serenity. And please do not let the people in your life—who themselves are dying of exhaustion and do not know how to rest—be your role models. Let sloths be your role models. Or koalas. Or any animal or plant. Please.

Bless your life and our world with your peak you. Healing miracles happen when you rest. Not just in you. In our web of life. It is time for us to be free people. It starts with rest. Bless you. Bless all your relations. May your spirit roam beautifully tonight.

YOU CAN TAKE OFF your suffer-ring. It was an unwise engagement anyhow.

YOU NEED NOT PUT SO MUCH pressure on yourself to have fun. To do things and go places. Without those expectations, you can relax into peace. Let peace decide what you do. It may be nothing at all. Well done.

If you want a new kind of peace and wellness, it may help to try a new kind of doing. Do less. Feel and release your anxiety, guilt, and shame about not doing. As those clouds clear, you may open up to an inner sky that feels so good you want to do less for the rest of your life. You will still be doing, though your doing will be rooted in wellness, so it will bear more fruit, more flowers, more life.

Doing less can dissolve your stress and refresh your energy. It can be medicine for your tiredness and tenderness. Be patient. Give doing less a chance. As you befriend it, it will introduce you to its best friends. One of those is Serenity.

WHEN HARMFUL THOUGHTS arrive, you can always say *Hey, I'm living here. Do you mind?*

REACH DEEP INSIDE yourself and touch your feeling of unworthiness. Hold it until it cries. It has been waiting all your life to be held by you. Only you.

Most of us live our lives carrying a stowaway. A feeling that we are not good enough. That we do not deserve better. That our soul desires are not meant to happen to people like us. Over time, this feeling calcifies into an identity, which becomes the cage in which we live. One of the ways this happens is through a fear that if we show our true self to the world, we will be laughed at, rejected, scorned. We feel the herd will banish us. But by living in this fear, we banish ourselves. From our true life. The one we are called for.

Living in your sacred, ancestral truth has the power to inspire others to set themselves free into their truths. A tender place exists deep inside you. A feeling of unworthiness. It may have many roots, many causes. What matters is being honest that this feeling lives in you. And that you see how it causes you to hold back, to give away your power and light, to stay in your cage, sabotaging the offering you could be making to the world.

Worthiness is a vibrational voice of permission and daring. Only you can keep it alive in you. If anything needs your attention, it is your feeling and story and identity of unworthiness. Dear soul, you cannot increase your worth. You were conceived and born and will always be priceless and qualified. You are a butterfly on the ground saying *I wish I could fly.*

You do not have to be someone else to manifest your own soul yearning. It is your soul. Your yearning. Your endowment of dreams. You are the only one who can make you feel worthy. Hold yourself with so much Love.

I AM WORTHY can be the most nutritious part of your daily diet. Shed your old identity and reveal who you really are. If you show us, some will be discomforted because they are living in their own cage. But you will inspire them toward the door. And maybe, one day, they will feel worthy, too.

YOUR PAIN CAN BECOME so familiar that you mistake it for your home, even as it causes you to suffer. BeLoved soul, do not renew this lease. A better home awaits you.

AS SOON AS YOU SAY *I am*, you aren't. What you name changes by the naming. Even without naming, you change. You are a boulder, and you are a river. But even a boulder is always changing.

YOUR PAIN CONTAINS a secret: your next chrysalis. All the chrysalises after. And the ultimate outcome of all those clothing changes: The fullness of you.

DO NOT BETRAY your own nature. Your feelings are a gift if you honor them. Let them show you what is healthy and what is not. Do not clench them. Let them move through, a wild flock of knowing, and be on their way. No more shame for the way you feel this life. Swim through that ocean to the coral reef of a beautiful condition. The best time to be deeply moved is while you are alive. Look, you are right on time.

YOU WERE BORN FOR THIS time on earth. Greed, materialism, power, control, and oppression are failed ways of life. But if you have a caring heart, and if you can summon a life that serves the collective, your services will always be in demand. And you will be fulfilled beyond your dreams. Behold, a new era of freedom is upon us. In the end, compassion will inherit this earth.

LET'S YOU AND I learn each other down to the molecule. So that when your soul and my soul meet in another world, we will recognize the braille of what we wove.

EACH DAY IS ANOTHER glorious opportunity to take a nap. Wise cultures have long known the personal and collective life-giving powers of the siesta. Step up. Lie down. Peace out. Tune in. Approach your days not as opportunities to exhaust yourself, but as opportunities to rest yourself back to life. I wish you the priceless gift of restedness.

SLOW DOWN. Daily contemplation of life is a root for wellness, healing, and fulfillment. It is how you gather meaning and purpose. If you are rushing, you cannot see. If you cannot see, you crash into things. Breathe. Pause. Contemplate. Gather meaning. Welcome to your beautiful life.

IF YOU CAN RELEASE your knowledge, like a dandelion seed in the breeze, you will gain more knowledge than you can imagine. Its name shall be *Truth*.

TODAY I WILL WRITE poetry for you. You will be my poetry, writing me. Today is writing all of this poetry. Sun is rising again and again inside this day. Light has learned a new Love song. Now, beneath the shade tree with blossoms of purple fountains, I usher this river through. Now, with a tender breeze patting my face with the same Love your brown hands pat into the white belly of tortilla dough, now this joy moves through.

Life is a song soaked in beauty. Life is a dance with no rules. No hours. No curfew. Just callouses building and breaking open again. Just the mist in your eyes. Eyes of a forest fawn. Eyes of dew. Plunging eyes, swimming great lakes of soul. And your brown hands, supple and survived, your brown hands kneading dough, pleading

Love into bread, bread into Love, Love into hunger, into bodies browned by Love, into lives leaning against kind moments of Love.

And I taste the bread your Love has made. Sky sings inside my bones, inside my breath, in the streams streaming my blood. You wake my ancestors. Everything is drumming now. Drum song is a vibration melting away what is not life from my life.

Come, place your brown hand in my brown hand. Today, we walk the Red Road, earth like blushing coffee. We walk the hills, green and billowing. We walk beneath oaks and eucalyptus, redwoods whispering wild languages. We walk along creeks and lips of lakes. We walk a million sunrises. Watering all living things with tears of Grace. We walk Creation, kneeling to smell and stroke the smallest grain. The bread you make is the rising of Love in every soul it feeds. Earth Loves you, sainted one. Your brown hands are how this life holds itself. In Love.

LAWMAKERS DO NOT have the power to make laws. The people do. What the people allow, becomes law. What the people insist, becomes law. What the people refuse cannot become law. Law is not the reflection of lawmakers. It is a reflection of the people. This is why you and I must be well. So that we—the pueblo, the people— may determine ourselves in a sacred way.

YOUR JOY IS A FRAGRANCE. Be your own divine diffuser. You can fill any space with your own exclusive essential oil. Be a mood enhancer. Make them ask where you got the good stuff.

YOU ARE A WOMB for world peace. This is how much you matter. Consider the qualities of a womb that bears health and goodness. Consider that you are ground zero for a global outbreak of healing and harmony.

DEAR SOUL. Do not wait for others to celebrate you. You are alive. That is the celebration. We spend life waiting to be appreciated, understood, celebrated. All along, our entire being is appreciating, understanding, celebrating itself. Every cell, process, and system. This is how we heal, grow, adapt, and thrive. You are alive, dear one. Feel the divine applause.

IF YOU WALK THROUGH a magnificent sand dune, do you go about picking out which grains are worthy of your joy, or do you enjoy the sensation of walking a sand dune? This is how it is for Love moving through human beings.

CUANDO HAY el Amor, hay la vida.

When there is Love, there is life.

LOVE MOVES THROUGH your soul whispering *Forget all you know. Remember me.* Most often, it is our ideas that prevent Love from naturally flowing through our vessel. When we are obstructed, we suffer. When we flow, we are a divine music, a peace parade. May we release our beliefs and associations and return to our original river nature.

AS SHE SPENT TIME in the wind, she became wind-like: light, supple, easy. She looked at the stone people around her: hard, heavy, immovable. She chose again the company of wind.

SEASON YOUR PAIN. Make it gumbo. Serve souls your medicine broth. Your heart is a garden of spices. Share your flavor.

YOU HAVE MOVED all the way around the belly of the sun one more time. And you say you never get to do anything special.

TODAY IS YOUR CLAY. Shape your precious life.

SOMETIMES, THE MOST LOVING ACT you can do for yourself is to kill your own identity. Now that you are conscious of so much more than when you began, and hopefully more compassionate, start over from scratch with your idea of you. Dare new ingredients.

WHAT SEED does not have to break through dirt before it becomes the life of its dreams? Today, the soil and toil. Tomorrow, your phenomenal sky.

JOY IS POSSIBLE, sweet soul. Sometimes its fruit grows on the high branches. Do not be afraid to reach for it.

MAYBE YOU ARE NOT LONELY or bored. Maybe your soul is calling you. We have been socialized to misread our soul signals. Constant external stimuli has dulled our joy for simply being, breathing, reflecting. We used to be peace gatherers. Now we hoard anxiousness, yearn for peace, yet are so afraid to move through the curtain of release to arrive at peacefulness. Good news: Practice makes peaceful.

BUT, DEAR. Your heart is supposed to gush. That is what it is for. Waterfall ways.

YOUR ACHE TO CREATE is all the qualification you need. If it is in you, set it free. Claim it. Birth it. No more waiting. Your inspiration is not just for you. It is for the world.

HELLO, SOUL. I sure do cherish you.

- Things to say to yourself

YOU WERE BORN with a Loving heart. Your mission in life is to keep it.

BEHOLD YOUR LIFETIME of doubt: And yet still you have not proven there is a thing you cannot do.

YOUR HEART WAS YOUR FIRST DRUM. Your first, genius music. Are you still listening?

TO BE LONELY, although the most natural of things, is also to be a fish in a stream, grieving water. What you want, you are. When you stop wanting it and start being it, the weight of loneliness can become a boundless sky of peace that invites all the things you are lonely for.

MANY HUMANS will not see you for they have not seen themselves. All other living things will see you, all the way down to your soul. This is because they live a life of soul. If you want to be seen, start by seeing yourself. This will change your aura and ways. In turn, others may notice you seeing you and figure maybe they ought to take a closer look.

BE VERY CAREFUL how you talk to yourself. It becomes your life. Words are seeds. When you say and think them, you plant, water, and sun them. Then they obey.

YOUR LIFE IS A sacred path forever lined with voices saying *Come this way*. What is a successful life? When you stay faithful to your path.

LOVE'S SACRED FIRE does not bargain. It burns into the truth of everything. Throughout human history, radical change for justice and sacredness has come forward on the high, holy tide of Lovers. A tide so strong it roars itself from the deep to flood the world with its demand. No exception. Only Love.

FEAR IS A CON ARTIST. Faith carries you home. Both say *Follow me*. Choose wisely.

YOU EXIST. Be in awe of that. It can help chase anxiety away.

LOVE LIKE YOU LOVE breeze on a hot day. No possession. Just gratitude.

YOUR SOUL IS A NUDIST. No more masks of fear. Just the bare, beautiful breath of Love. The nakedness that matters happens on the inside. Reveal your astounding heart and soul.

YOUR JOY IS a wild thing. Make sure to let it roam.

LET YOUR TEARS come, mighty and true. They can wash your whole life clean. Your tears are your own personal baptismal water.

JUST BECAUSE YOU miss them does not mean you are supposed to be with them. Do not let your pain confuse you, dear one. The pain of separation often is a divine gift that burns you back to yourself. A wildfire that clears away the old to ready your soil for what is new. Take a deep, Loving breath and move through to the other side. Something your soul has always wanted is waiting. Not someone. Something called Peace.

YOU ARE NOT HERE for war. The world is drowning in war. You are here for Love. We have not known your Love before. Every morning when you wake: *I am here for Love*. When you go to sleep: *I am here for Love*. When anger flares or hurt pierces: *I am here for Love*. When you feel loneliness, sorrow, pity, or fear: *I am here for Love*.

How do you find yourself, stay yourself, bless yourself, bless all living things? Saturate your soul in your reminder, your mantra, your sacred song and its only verse: *I am here for Love*.

WHAT MAKES YOUR soul flower? Live in that sunlight. What a gift it is that you have the freedom and power to garden your own life. Regardless the conditions.

WE ALL HAVE MEDICINE for the world. Choose to share your healing power.

NO MATTER HOW YOU pray, pray more. If your prayer is a smile, smile deeper. If you pray by singing, sing with every breath. Soak in more sunlight. Mantra more moonlight. Ache more joyfully. Hug more Lovingly. Apply your kindness more freely. Believe in your own soul. Make silence your choir. Carve out space for peace. Sculpture Grace. See souls more clearly. Ordain yourself a healer. Be a dreamcatcher. Beautify your spirit. Shed your identity. Dive into your divine ocean. Stay there.

LOOK AT LIFE through a Lover's eyes and see that all of life is a separation and joining. Sleeping and waking. Bloom and fade. Hurt and healing. No one is exempt from this divine parade. You might as well rejoice.

NO ONE ASKS THE SUN why it rises or shines. You do not have to explain why you Love. You are Love, made human. Shine on.

A SMILE IS NOT just a facial expression. It is a sunrise for the souls it touches.

LOVE SO passionately that nothing else has room to grow in the garden of your heart.

HOW TO MOVE THROUGH CHANGE: Let your leaves fall. Grow new roots. Change colors as necessary to absorb the energy of your present moment. Take rest when needed. Which is often. Embrace the solitude of companionship, and the companionship of solitude. Change organically, not according to social opinion. Remain open to what goes and what arrives. Discern all of it. Cry good. Take another nap.

A BEAUTIFUL LIFE forever blooms with healing. Do not be ashamed of your healing journey. Be grateful you have found it. Cherish it like a new life. For it is one. In every breath.

WE CELEBRATE the beautiful creation of art, music, and dance. But a sacred art lives in us that we often neglect to practice or celebrate. No matter what suffering we encounter in life, we are free and empowered to deepen our own wondrous art of breathing. Breathe through your pain. Breathe peace back into your soul. Breathe your dreams into being.

Your breathing is an affirmation to your living system that it is alive, safe, strong, able. It brings you into union with all that is. Breathe trauma clouds out into the sky of healing. Breathe your memories along into a sweeter meadow. Breathe your spirit into focus, swelling it with health and vitality. Breathe your intrinsic song awake within. Breathe the poetry of you into your bones.

Your breath resurrects you. Carries you. Clarifies you. Replants you in fertile ground. Breathe beautifully, dear soul. Your breathing is a miracle, a paradise, an art you may forever grow.

SKY ALWAYS waters itself first. Take deep care of you. Without soil, how can you grow a garden? You are the soil for your every relationship. Nurture yourself and you are a fertile soil. Neglect yourself and your soil cannot bring forth harvest. Your soil is worth the investment.

DO SOMETHING TODAY unannounced to the world. See how it feels just to exist. No performance. No attention or judgment. No applause or reaction. Just you. Savoring this miracle of being you.

YOU, LOVING YOU. Your greatest romance. The one that makes all your other Love bonds more beautiful. You with you. This togetherness is the soul of your whole life. How you are with you is how you are with the world. Want Love's fire? Light it for yourself. Illuminate your aura. Then dance to the flames until your glory tears flow out. Until all that you feel for you is the most awesome gratitude for being you, bearing you, witnessing you. Testify. Your every heartbeat is a sacred word, a Love letter from you to you. You cannot be Loved more completely than by you. Rejoice. It was always you.

PRIVACY IS YOUR own personal matchmaker. Your date tonight? Your beloved soul.

SATURATE YOURSELF with goodness, wellness, rest, and Love. Soak yourself until your overflow waters the world. You do not have to be a drought. You can be a waterfall so gushing that every arid soul you touch becomes a newborn ocean.

YOUR LIFE IS NOT A SERIES OF DAYS. It is a river of miracles. When you see the miracles in every moment, you flood your heart with awe, thanks, and praise. Worry dissolves. Fear fades away, replaced by glory rays. Sing. Sing praise.

WHEN YOU LEARN TO SAVOR YOUR SOUL, your whole life becomes a delicacy.

THE REVOLUTION BEGAN with your first breath.

Is your life or world not as you wish? Good news: You were born with the power to enact the change you now want. Which is why you want it. It is your destiny. No need to wait on age, development, degrees, experience, good fortune, or timing. Your natural power is the greatest power you will ever hold. You brought with you into this world a persona and presence never before seen. Your essence is unprecedented. Overthrow unjust ways. End generational harm. Heal your life, and so the world. You are the prophecy. Do not wait. Need backup? Recruit your own soul. Your warriors will follow.

LET LOVE RAISE YOU. Not like you raise a child. Like you raise a mountain. Love can awaken all your ancestors. Grow into your power, dear soul. Peace is waiting.

YOU DO NOT HAVE TO live your life like an algorithm. Feel things. Get drenched. Fire walk. Each moment is an aperture. Look and see every miracle strung on a loom of miracles inside the miracle of this moment. If you feel no awe, you are not alive. Ideas and ideologies do not make you alive. Only passion can do that. Regress yourself into a seed so you can be born again. Relive the journey of birth and infancy. When your leaves dry and brown, drop them. Always be ready to bud. Find volcanoes and offer yourself to their miasmic mouths. You are not a single river. You are countless waters. Hear their honey hymns.

DEEP COMPASSION in you may leave you feeling guilt as you guide others to their difficult truth. Remember, you are not the splinter in their body. Nor the pain it causes. Nor the hand pulling it out. You are the light that helps them see the splinter, the source of the pain, its damage, and their own hand arriving to do salvation work. You are not the cause of their suffering. You are a breeze moving in the direction of the end of their suffering. You do not create the way, or determine the way. You are but a breeze, benign and benevolent. The way water washes a seed along to its new and fertile ground.

COMPASSION IS AN ART. Paint outside the lines. Burn up all your rules for caring. Care without borders. Save your heart by setting it free.

HOW BRAVE TO LOVE in this world. How absolutely essential. What if you discovered that Love is the very air of life? Would you breathe it? Love is not soft, a weakness. It is brave, an apex roar in the wilderness. When you are fully in Love, no predators may encroach on your territory. They catch your scent and flee. In Love, you are gapingly vulnerable and yet invincible, a divine paradox worth musing. Stop Loving, and see how long you live. Your soul's oxygen is Love. Do not hold your breath. A Lover is the bravest soul of all.

DO NOT RUN FROM the mountain. It is your way out. Climb it. Give your challenges beautiful names. Then they become your blessing, your revelation, your beautiful life.

IF YOU TREAT your life as gently as you would a baby, your sweet soul just might blossom.

YOU WISH someone would treat you the way you want to be treated. Go first.

YOU CAN FLY your emotions like a kite or drag them like an anchor. The gift of life is that you get to choose. Even a heavy swell can be ridden to happiness. Our journey is about learning to be in a gentle relationship with our emotions, and not to be a slave to them. Freedom is our soulful heritage. Inner kindness one of our most precious legacies. Wishing you the lightness of a cool summer breeze and the emotional habit to stay aloft in the sky of your peace.

SELF-LOVE IS HOW you introduce yourself to the world. Make the right impression. Self-Love is not complicated. Be kind. To all that you are. To all that is. Self-Love is a habit. Get your reps in. Self-Love has no limit. When you feel you have reached its depths, go deeper. May your self-Loving thoughts breed freely and populate your entire life with beauty. How you feel about the *We* that is also you. Nurture that garden.

EACH GENERATION has a duty to reckon with its particular insanity. In the hopes that it may offer this world a new kind of being sane. You come into this world with your own unique way of seeing. Life dirties and obscures your vision. Your sacred daily task is to keep your vision clear. Suffering is a generational rope whose strands are woven of fear. Rare are those souls willing to let go of this rope, and by letting go, to become medicine for themselves and all of Creation.

DO NOT SPEND YOUR LIFE counting those who have wronged you. Spend your life counting those who have been kind to you. Their kindness is your currency. It still lives in you, swirling, making the sweetest medicine. Who is kind to you? Those are your people. Hopefully, you are one of them.

HOW MANY SEEDS must you plant before you Love yourself? Stop counting. Keep planting. Your beautiful life is all about the sowing, dear one. One day, you unbend your weary back, stand tall, and looking all around you, you see: What used to be barrenness is a divine, lush wilderness whose beauty brings you weeping to your knees. No more counting. Just the joy of seeding. Kind thought after kind thought, you shed your old heavy skin and burdensome mentality, and come forth anew, revealing the sensual grace, the astounding light that is your phenomenal joy.

OPPRESS NO LIVING THING. Especially yourself. Freedom is not what you gather. It is what you release. Give away your fear, your false ideas, your need to please. Burn your bindings in Love's sacred fire. Dance naked in moonlight. Roar at the wilderness. It will roar back at your mating call. Cut the kite strings holding your soul to the slavery of conformity and habit. Cancel your memberships. Dare to wake and live. Surrender your conformed sanity. You are a ceremony. Burn. Bake. Sing. Soar.

OUR HOPE lies in the truth that we possess ancestral memory. Our spirit existed before our birth into this world. It carries within it inherent, intrinsic goodness and wellness, which we can retrieve if we care to go back far enough into our journey. Back to our conception, back to our ancestors, back into the Love we are that existed long before our childhood trauma. We must choose to believe that our essence is wellness. If we choose to believe otherwise, unwellness will be our fate. If it feels like no memory of wellness exists inside, still we have the power to work from faith, until wellness becomes a memory again. Endless blessings.

CALL OUT YOUR BLESSINGS every day. They will answer, breed, and grow. If you are consumed with what is right in your life, you do not have the focus, energy, or time to be consumed with what you feel is wrong. Your harvest will be predictable, sufficient, and pure. This is how joy behaves: Fill your whole soul with gratitude. Leave room for nothing else. Saturate your inner ocean. Walk in Grace. Grace will show you what it is made of.

WHEN YOU ARE TRUE to yourself, the joy you feel is your every ancestor hugging you. They were not perfect as people. As ancestors, their every hope and dream for you is divine.

SHE RECLAIMED her wholeness privately. Breath by brave breath, she rose in Love.

Dearly BeLoved... If your self-esteem depends on social attention and compliments, it isn't self-esteem. It is social esteem. Self-esteem is a private gardening. Not a public offering. Bring spring to your soul. All your favorite flowers are waiting to bloom.

SOUL CHANGE births social change. If you want it, you have to go in and get it. What you want the world to be, you must be. Change your soul climate, and you change the world. Be hopeful. This is a world of souls, and you, beLoved, are a soulful thing.

DO NOT COVER UP. Your soul is showing. In a world of masks, facades, and eclipses, where so many are suffocating beneath their layers, you can offer a rare reprieve. A dual blessing to you and others: your truth. An organic medicine that tends to wake those who walk in sleep. True courage is letting yourself be seen.

WHAT SPRING DOES to a meadow, do that to your life. Do not say you cannot. We have seen the light of your *soulrise*. Believe in your shine.

REST. EVEN WHEN you are doing, you can do so restfully. Be aware of the tension and anxiousness you are holding. Release it through your gentle breath and be at rest. Rest your bones. Your cells. Your many rivers. Live restfully and everything improves. We have been duped into believing we are allergic to rest, glorifying our exhaustion. Whether or not your diet is plant-based, make sure your life is rest-based. Be like a morning flower at its best. Rest.

EVERY DAY IS A SERMON. And that sermon is Love. Let Love be your minister, message, sanctuary, psalm, and song.

HOLD YOUR HEART tonight like a newborn. It is. You are. Your heart and life are so preciously tender because in every wondrous moment, you are newly born. Rejoice in your brave adventure.

THE ANXIETY LIVING IN YOU is only a guest. It is okay for you to usher it out the door.

Self-care is remembering your true identity, which is Peace. You don't have to host everything that wants to overstay its visit. Especially invasive species like fear and anxiety. Show your deepest hospitality to your native energy: the serene aura of Love. With patient, Loving work in the garden of your life, you can reclaim peace within your soul.

IN THE SPACES between Loving breaths, she gently found her song and self.

Your breathing is everything, you see? It is how you are kind to your native land (heart and soul).

DO NOT MAKE A HOME of victimhood. The structure always collapses. Your healing power is a superior shelter. Move in. Redecorate. Be stubborn about peace. Determine to have a beautiful life now. No matter what. Live in that joy. Make your wellness a continuous housewarming party.

YOU ARE A NATURAL WONDER of the world. No need to seek greatness. Behold yourself. When you fully realize how wondrous you are, you will want to spend the rest of your life traveling. Inside your soul. Peace is your passport to visiting you. Deep breath, beLoved soul. You have arrived. Now another grateful breath. Keep arriving.

SOME DAYS you cross the desert, and thirst. Some days the wide blue sea, yearning for land. Needs change as life changes. Pay close attention to your soulful cravings. They say something about the landscape, the road ahead, and the conditions for which you might want to prepare. Your soul is a ceremony of life itself. Be in it. Give praise, sing, and dance.

THE PROBLEM OF SOCIETY is a problem of the soul. Like a polluted river, what begins in the soul arrives into society. What churns in society arrives back to the soul.

LOOK UP AT THE ENDLESS SKY. Your Love is so much bigger. Loving kindness is your only legacy that matters. Give your whole life to it. Love must be manifest to have meaning in this world. Kindness is that manifestation. All your titles and acclaim fade in time. What remains forever is the warm mist of mercy and grace you leave inside of souls. Your heart's outward ovation makes you immortal.

KEEP GOING. You are almost there. Where? Your next breath. Sometimes you are left with no choice but to live from breath to breath. And sometimes you choose to live like this because doing so brings you all the way alive. A single breath can be the most extraordinary experience. A close brush with the miraculous Divine. When you realize it is Creation that is breathing, and you are its breath, your whole life changes. You realize you are an instrument for a phenomenal music and dance. Therefore, you must be phenomenon. And all around you, the inspiration and muse.

YOU ARE A DIAMOND OF FREEDOM forged by ages of oppression. Now, it is your turn to shine. Behold what emerges from the fire, stronger than the fire. Friction and pressure made Love to you deep in the earth of your moments and experiences, deep in the bedrock of your pain and trauma, harm and loss, hope and prayer. Your tears were the water that mixed with stone to grind you into this luminance you are and do not fully recognize. Your emotions now are grand canyon rivers of your soul calling out to life itself: *Come see and share in this glory I am.*

ALL THE JOY you have ever felt or dreamed of would like your permission to hold a reunion in your heart. Go ahead, host the party.

PEACE IS AN INSIDE JOB. Do not depend on anyone else to give it to you. Nobody can give it to you. Nobody can take it away. That is the beauty of peace: It lives inside your freedom.

HER BEST DAYS weren't behind her or ahead of her. They were inside her, and would be, forever more.

SHE SMILED SO MUCH because she finally understood: She was free. She always would be. No matter what.

Freedom is a birthright and a determination to live free. Do not just keep your head up. Keep your whole soul up, too. Breathe all the way. Live all the way. Believe all the way. A beautiful life is yours. Decidedly.

SHE BURNED THE SHAME planted in her, the worry and sadness, and planted a new crop: unapologetic joy.

Sometimes, you have to get rambunctious, brazen, liberated with your joy. Sometimes, you have to burn all the old crops, turn the ground, dance your ceremony, and plant new seeds. Patience is key to fruitful farming. Have faith. Keep planting. Watering. Loving. You. Back to life. Back to your original radiance.

MEASURE YOUR LIFE in breaths. Then you will realize how blessed you are.

WRITE IT. CHANT IT. Pray it. Sing it. Say it. Dance it. Cry it. Laugh it. Loud it. Proud it. Whisper it. Rewind it: *I am worthy of Loving myself. I am worthy of Loving myself. I am worthy. I am Love. I am Love. I am Love.*

THE GREATEST JOURNEY she ever took was to heal herself.

You can go around the world a thousand times. Until you go inside your soul and make peace and Love, you have not actually gone anywhere. Nor have you witnessed your greatest wonder. You can learn to cherish healing. It can become your precious craft. Your patient poetry. Your lifelong Love affair.

WHEN YOU SEE SOMEONE who has good light, thank them for it. It helps them keep the light on.

When you find a soul on fire with Loving light, do not just bask. Add your goodness to the flames. This illumination work is a tribal endeavor. Seeing the sacred in another soul is a ceremony all by itself. Weaving gratitude blankets is how we heal.

SELF-LOVE—communal, ancestral Love activated in you—is the best kind of gardening. Take a beautiful breath and get down in the dirt.

HOW KIND CAN YOU BE to yourself in your next moment? That is the journey. Growth is not a sand dune. It is a sand grain.

LEARNING THE DIFFERENCE between freedom and self-destruction is everything. Your life depends on it. Just because you can does not mean you should. Self-Love is a maturity of choice. And for those deciphering adulthood: Freedom is not doing whatever you want. It is doing your duty. If your duty is unclear, you are not yet free.

UNTIL YOU KNOW YOUR soul's truest song, you cannot possibly know music.

DO YOU WANT PEACE? Want truth more. Then you will have peace, dear one. Truth is a climate. Learn to live there, and all things become a kind of ease. Let the debates and arguments inflame around you. Stay in the peace water soaking up Grace. For your sake. For all of us.

WHATEVER SOIL DOES with a seed, solitude can do with your soul. Do not be afraid to be with yourself. You hold all that you've been yearning for. More than that. A birthing exists unlike what you can find outside yourself. Its glory is the difference between wild-picked fresh berries and store-bought decay labeled as fruit. Patience may not be popular these days, but it is potent. If you take a dose of quietude and stillness, first your mind may rebel. But be assured, your soul will already be dancing. Be with the *You* of you. Let the divine music play.

ON YOUR HEALING JOURNEY, being true to your soul means the difference between a flashlight and sunlight. The way forward can be dark as moonless night. Stay true to you. Illuminate your road.

A SENSITIVE, VOLUMINOUS, reverberating soul is a deep drum. One that when touched releases its profound holdings, exuding a powerful, healing song. Find your deep drums and boom with them.

GRACE AND GRATITUDE are superfoods. Get your diet right. Feed yourself this daily bread. Eat and drink and breathe your blessings. This is especially a priority for healers and tender-hearted creatures who feel every tremble.

I HAVE GATHERED so much Love. Won't you join me for this feast? No one leave the table. What we eat and drink has no end. After this night, we will never stop singing.

I HAVE WITNESSED a miracle. Two days ago, on the branch of an olive tree outside my kitchen window, a hummingbird chose to make its nest. Yesterday the hummingbird birthed an egg in that nest. A tiny, delicate alabaster egg. And so, life again. A tree. A bird. A weaving. A birthing. This ought to be enough for awe and wonder. For bowing down and looking up. In praise.

LOVE IS THE SOUL'S WATER, infinite and everywhere. Yet we suffer an intolerable drought. We are the only living things that choose to suffer from an absence that does not exist. You are a fountain, dear one. Pour and drink.

BURN YOUR IDENTITY in a caring fire. Let a new one grow fresh each day. Don't get lost in who you think you are. Break free of that old cave. Go wandering in the woods. Find a waterfall. Leap from its cliff into the water below. Get soaked in something new. Your true identity has no edges or outlines. It goes on and on. Be willing to shred your labels and signposts so you can build a fresh sky and roam it all the way.

DRINK YOUR DAILY TEA. Immerse in the boiling, the pouring, the steaming, the drinking. Actual tea or not, have a ceremony for your peace. Ceremony keeps you close to you, and stills your waters for the moments to come.

PAY CLOSE ATTENTION to those whose presence in your life feels like pure soul, no agenda or need. Flow there.

PRIVACY IS A WOMB for your sacred things. Let your jewels have their intimate time to become finished jewels.

A RIVER DEMANDS that if you are to know it, you must go beneath its surface and feel and be soaked in its depth. So, too, your soul.

THE CLEAREST MIRROR you will ever look into is your own soul. Look inside. The best lighting and truest reflection live there.

KINDNESS IS NOT a favor to others. It is a favor to yourself. A soul massage. Indulge yourself often.

SHE BREATHED IT ALL OUT. Peace came back in.

YOU AND SPRING are kindred spirits. Believe in your power to bloom. What was, was. Your flowering awaits. You are seed, earth, sky, water, sun. Faith and patience are your tools. Stay in your ceremony. Breathe, dear one. Blooming is a delicate thing.

WHATEVER STORY you are telling yourself, that is your life. The beauty of this is that you are the storyteller. You write the drafts and the final script. It is never too late. Once upon a time, there was a *You*. There still is.

YOUR WHOLE LIFE changes when you realize that your eternal beauty doesn't live in your appearance. It lives in your kindness. Kindness is a beauty product. Not the kind that conceals you. The kind that reveals you. Here's to your continuous makeovers.

ONE DAY YOU WILL EXPRESS FOUR WORDS. And these four words will set you free. The words are:

This Is My Truth.

You will speak, write, sing, dance, laugh, act on, remember, celebrate, feel, dream, and live these words in endless ways. These four words will clarify your relationships, illuminate who means what in your life.

These four words will steady your soul and introduce the false you to the true you. In the presence of the true you, the false you will grow tentative and begin to fade away. Wounds in you will tenderize, then transform like snow in a warm sky.

The healer you are will awaken and stretch its translucent muscles. *This Is My Truth* will be your ointment, herb, tonic, and ceremony.

You will *pray This Is My Truth* when life's tide roars against your cliffs and the pain of your tenderness extracts grains from your shore. *This Is My Truth* will fortify you in the storm. It will be your reassuring rainbow after.

Some misty mornings you will go walking into the woods seeking these four words. And you will find them growing wild in a clearing rimmed with tall, sage trees. And you

217

will kneel in the soft moss of these four words. And sun bars will bless your skin as you gently pluck petals from these four words and place them in your mouth. And the softness of their offering will soothe what trembles in you.

You will learn to stay in wild meadows where these four words grow, and you will stay even as the world's unwellness swells around you, threatening to erase these four words.

And you will chant these four words. And you will chant until they become your native language. Until these four words rearrange your molecules and juice your atoms with their airy essence.

One day, a mountain will rise in the ocean of your soul. And it will be these four words. *This Is My Truth* will be your island, your oasis, your paradise. Your power. *This Is My Truth* will be your mating call. Kindred souls will flock to this song you usher, this aroma that is your atmosphere.

All the family and friends and unfamiliar souls threatened by your four words, and offended, disappointed, angered, and left unhinged and unmoored by the blaspheming reality of their own missing four words, all these souls will finally lie down on the soft savanna woven of your four words and they will weep a deep surrender. Their four words, already in them a seed, shall be inspired by your four words and your living of them. Their four words will stir, then sprout, and this great valley of souls will begin a legendary healing.

You will sit and rest your back against an old tree younger than the youngest sun. You will ease into sacred conversation with all of Creation. And Creation will ask *What is your offering*? And your sweetened soul will

218

gather its eons of Love-harvest and it will answer *I shall offer this. This Is My Truth*. And Creation will open and receive your offering. Your truth will open and flow profoundly into all things. And your four words will live forever in the breeze, the most subtle dance of pollen and sunlight birthing life, birthing life, birthing all this life.

ARE YOU A LIVING THING? Then you, dear, must water yourself. Love is that water. You must breathe. Peace is that breath. And you must rest. Release your wanting. Know the bliss of being.

DO NOT LIVE OUTSIDE YOUR JOY and call yourself homeless. Move into your joy and make yourself at home.

THE DISTANCE between pain and peace can be measured in choices. One choice to heal after another. Breath by breath. Hope by hope. Tear by tear. Truth by truth. The way home can be arduous. Yet its air is composed of a gentleness to yourself. A continuous forgiving of your imperfection. A starlight of faith to guide you. Then, once you have arrived home to your whole being, you see that the way was worth it. More than that. It was the only way that could end at the garden of your sacred peace.

THE WAY FRUIT RIPENS from stone-hard to soft gift. Blueprint for a healing heart and the sugar it gathers.

WHEN YOU KNOW you are whole, and live as though you are whole, you make your every ancestor smile. Make them smile. Revolt against what wants you to live in pieces. Live in peace. Gather your entire being, all your meadows and mountains and moons and majesty, and live in that forever. Remember, the revolution began with your first breath.

THIS IS HOW you will bathe yourself tonight. Fill your bed with kind thoughts. Sleep in them. Epsom salts have nothing on the kindness in which you soak your soul. Be your greatest Lover.

IN THE END, life comes down to two questions: *What do you consider sacred? How do you treat your sacred things?*

May you consider all things sacred. Especially yourself. Living sacredly is a cure for ailments of the heart and soul. If no one has taught you this, fortunately teachers live in you and all around you in the natural world. Find them by finding Love in you. Love will introduce you to your teachers. Who will show you yet deeper into the sacred ways of Love. Ahó.

PAIN IS A TUNING instrument. Use it to tune your soul to peace. Pain is the soul's determination to surface. To be free. Follow the pain in you, not toward the nightmare your fear imagines, but in the divine direction your soul, through pain, wants to take you. Do not walk your pain-dog where you think you want to go. Let your pain-dog walk you where it wants to go. Its senses are keener than yours. It knows where the clean water is, the good food, the safe places to rest or play. Peace is an eternal song calling to you. Use your pain to harmonize with peace.

WHEN WALKING THROUGH the woods of your life, do not follow your fear obediently. It often runs away from your salvation. Follow the pure Love in you that began before you began. Follow your inheritance as a soul of life. Do this and your walk through the woods will beget a richness of meaning whose beauty makes you cry.

A POET IS ONE whose soul is irretrievably open to Love's river. One who releases the music of that sacred water. This music is everywhere. Even a sigh is poetry.

SHE USED TO GATHER her favorite flowers. Now she is her favorite flower. This is the gardening soul work can do. We Love what blooms in nature because it is a reflection of what blooms in us. Beauty recognizes beauty. See and sing to your own.

DO NOT BE AFRAID, dear one, of platonic intimacy and caring. Love is a sacred blanket woven in many ways.

EVERYONE WANTS YOU once everyone wants you. They don't really want you. They want to be a part of the wanting. And before everyone wants you, very few will want you, for what they really want is the wanting. Rarely will you be seen and therefore cherished for who you really are, whether or not you are wanted. See yourself. Cherish yourself. Want yourself. So you may be free.

WARRING AGAINST INNER UNWELLNESS, self-harm, and harmfulness to the world, a true warrior wages an uncommon courage in ascending to enlightened grace, determined for kindness and honor with all things.

SOMETIMES, LOVE IS NOT a person. Sometimes Love is a thought you choose. And your soul says *Please, dear, can you be kinder to me? Water me with good words. With meaning like spring water. With sunlight even in the storm. I need meadows of warm thoughts. Peaceful translations of your life. This is how I like to be Loved.*

LOOKING FOR A SOULMATE? Your dear soul *is* your mate. Mission accomplished. None more perfect, more faithful, more fulfilling, more foundational for all your other relations. Stay in your ceremony of ceremonies. Which is your soul. All your true mates will find you.

I AM WORTHY. Sing this to your soul, in the shower, in bed, in your dreams, when crying, when dying, birthing, reaching, breaching, aching, grieving, fearing, flying. Sing this song until your soul sings it back to you.

BECOME POPULAR and you might be known for a hundred years. Become a living soul of truth, and your light will burn for eternity in the hope of living things.

LET US SINK OUR SOULS into the soil of truth and grow an untamed life. Beautiful soul, remember, your existence is a rebellion against the odds. You are already an outlier. An exception. An unexpected thing. You have nothing to which to tame yourself. *Untame* your coiled condition. You are finest in your feral form.

YOU NEED NOT SEEK MIRACLES. You are one. Live like it.

BeLoved, do not treat your life as a long homework assignment, a chore, a burden. It is a miracle that you were conceived, that you survived gestation and birth. That you have seen so many suns and moons, and have known the intensities of pain and laughter, each returning you to your soul. Your very existence is a blasphemy against the void. Grasp the glory of your life. Sing it. For it is a song.

YOU, BELOVED, are your own sweet cure for loneliness. Really, really be with yourself. Make the introduction. The ache is your soul saying *Please, at last, give me to me. I want myself.*

If you can learn to want yourself, and then to give yourself what you want, want will disappear. And you will know peace. If you feel that you are not worth wanting you, then perhaps you have not yet known you. For if you know you, you will want you. And if you want you, it is only because you know you.

The resolution is in moving beyond delusion, your inherited ideas of you, and entering the realm of your pure soul that cannot be defined. If you please, I will say this another way: You are a song who wants music. Remember the song and you will have your music.

BE KIND, SACRED, and true. Make your ancestors blush.

EVERY BREATH YOU TAKE, your ancestors breathed first. Give thanks. For their breathing. For the sacred air they passed on to you. For the way you give it back to them. By breathing beautifully and living a fully inflated life.

THE POETRY OF YOUR LIFE is written in the ink of how you make souls feel. Please leave a beautiful calligraphy as your legacy.

GATHER. OFFER. PRAY. Drum. Sing. Dance. Rest. Revolt. Remember. This is how to be human again.

CAREFUL WHERE YOU lay down your dreams. You don't want to misplace them. They can scatter from neglect. Stay in your spirit garden. Grow roots there alongside everything that calls to you.

YOU WILL KNOW THOSE SOULS who drench themselves in the Divine. Their humility and light are clues. They know they are nothing. Therefore they shine with everything.

WHEN YOU ARE IN PAIN, even beauty can hurt. You may resent those who exude beauty, who speak and write of beauty, who offer kindness on the side of the road, and who want to pour compassion in your cup.

When you are in pain, you can be lost in a story of suffering that quickly comes to define you. Anything or anyone who is a reflection of a different kind of story becomes a threat to the tight grip you have on your idea of who you are, what the world is.

When you feel this angry, desperate surging in you, see if you can let it sweep you into a tide pool of calmer water. Breathe. Hold your heart. Acknowledge that, at this time, beauty is hard for you to bear. In your acknowledgment lives a medicine. A seed of surrender to the truth of your immediate season. This surrender is, all by itself, a healing ground. A beginning of a journey through which you become the beauty others cannot yet bear.

IF YOU WERE YOUR FAVORITE FLOWER, what would be your favorite kind of human? Be that. Make a flower happy today.

BE A FINDER, seer, sayer of beautiful things.

GIVE OF YOUR RICH LIFE. Hoarding your blessings causes loneliness, too.

DO NOT WORRY about how your offering will fair in a world of so many offerings. Yes, the world has more bread and more bakers than ever. More mouths to feed, too. Have faith in what comes through you. Let it be pure. There will always be those who hunger for bread only you can bake.

DO NOT JUDGE ART by the fame of the artist. Don't judge it at all. Open your *everything* to it. This is how you enrich yourself and learn to be an artist in the way you stir up meaning from even the most mundane mud puddles of your life.

SAY I AM POETRY. Say I am medicine. Gathering of old sap. Warm breaking of bread. What the owl sees. Precision of blood. You ask what I am. Say I am nothing. Let silence sing my song.

BE PATIENT with yourself. Each moment is your first time. You are always new. Being hard on yourself is a habit you learned from others being hard on you, hard on themselves. Be a revolutionary. Try gentleness.

OUT BEYOND the lemon orchards, I go to the valley. To the mountain. To pray. To praise. To let my spirit resume its poetry. Each time, the muses wait there for me. Breeze, sky, earth, water, sun-fire, hawks on the wind, coyotes up to mischief, a bold silence that speaks to me. These muses remind me: Creator is a poet. I, a single lyric wanting to be held close and sung purely by the Song.

THE BLADES OF THIS discontent find their line across the soft moss of a tenured heart, and sink in. Only the yellow yarrow waving in the dry valley and on the hills can dull the edges, sending the knife sliding helplessly over grateful tissue. Peace blossoms in clusters, from trees and shrubs, and even the water sings with new light. Above, sky is amused.

BE A SAFE PLACE for yourself. Be the safest place. Heal your thoughts, mind, heart, meaning, memories. Renovate your reactions. Learn how to sing to your tenderness. Rest more. Release. Release. Release. Make your inner oasis a lifelong creative project. Find joy in the labor.

NO MATTER HOW the pain got in you, it is your sacred calling to get it out. On the day you decide to no longer focus on who hurt you and choose to devote yourself to healing the hurt, you bless your ancestors. You bless your descendants. You bless every living thing. Healing means that much. It is a tremble in the intimate lagoon that becomes a mighty ripple through the ocean of existence. Your healing determines the world. This is how great you are.

ALL YEARNING is the soul saying *Come home to me*. You don't have to go home. You are home. You *are* your home. Stay. Unpack. Move around. Grow familiar. When you stop wandering, wanting, peace flowers inside. Once, you were homeless, anxious, and seeking. Now you are *homeful*. An endless sunrise in your soul.

IF YOU CAN SPEND all day doing nothing but filling your soul with joy, you have lived a fruitful day. Let being be enough.

START A RUMOR. Tell yourself you deserve to heal and be happy. Pass it on. If you are going to gossip, gossip about yourself. In your own mind. Make it good. Make it medicine.

YOU ARE THE ONLY ONE to have experienced every moment of your life. Remember this when people presume about your journey. Be at peace with your knowing. Trust it. Trust your truth. Make medicine from it. Gather your many seeds. Weave your blankets. Sing your songs. Dance and drum. Smudge yourself. Wade in the water. Shed your tears. Love deeper. Laugh harder. Remember. Release. Be an endless ceremony. All your relations. Ahó.

TAKE YOUR TIME. Get to know your pain. Once you become friends, it will trust your touch and change to fertile light, useful dark, and a passion for truth.

IMAGINE YOURSELF imagining yourself. Imagine this imagination beautifully.

Your lungs breathe air. Your heart breathes Love. Be sure to take your medicine. Know your design. Your nature is your medicine. Feed yourself what you hunger for. Become full, so you have something to share. Share, so you become full. Sing, so you have music in your life. Keep music in your life, so that you sing. If you want to feel peace, practice peace, then you will feel it. Imagine yourself imagining yourself. You are the thread of the very blanket you want to keep you warm. Weave your blanket. We are talking here about your life. Open the door and let it in. Be a good host. Let your life live in you. Feel it beautifully. It is your greatest miracle.

YOUR TENDER PLACES are gifts. They show you where your touch is needed. And how to touch. Here's to your tenderness. The soil it is. The blossoms it brings.

HEALING CAN BE a joyful thing. A wonderfully untidy personal art project. A hallelujah in your house of soul.

SPEND THIS SUMMER in the garden of your soul. You won't believe the blossoms.

I WOULD LIKE TO introduce myself. I am earth, water, fire, and wind. The four teachers and directions. Ancestor breath. Cradle for who comes next. I am memory and vision. The ocean in your tears. Your tears in the ocean. I am the impossible window and what you see through it. Purify yourself. Lay down your tobacco. Pray with your every molecule and cell. Enter this Love. What moon does to you tonight is what you must do to the world.

HEALER. Truth is your medicine. Even when truth is hard. Especially then.

LOVE IS HOW your heart breathes. It is a vital act and condition that keeps you alive. Make sure you are taking big, beautiful breaths.

IF YOU OPEN your sacred eyes wide enough, you see that in your social justice endeavors you are not striving against poverty and oppression, but against those who work to preserve poverty and oppression. Overcome their spirit and resistance, and poverty and oppression evaporate, for they are not the natural order of things. Life thrives when truly free.

IT IS AN ESSENTIAL JOURNEY to go from being a bird in the sky cawing *Look at me, look at me*! to drafting the high, hot winds singing *Look at we, look at we*!

As we experience union and communion, and soak ourselves in that phenomenal nature, anxiety, fear, and loneliness dissolve. Those are replaced by a wondrous peace, calm, openness, belonging, compassion, and humility of perspective wed to Love's enduring grace.

Experiencing yourself as all things grants a powerful and grounding life purpose. Souls living in oneness are free from the despairing insecurities of those consumed in their tight, frightened individualism. Gift yourself with dissolution. Live awed and illuminated by the miracle of *We*.

MAKE PEACE YOUR final homeland. Be that kind of immigrant. Be the one who leaves the cave of generational trauma and walks out into the paradise of wellness and ease. Taste a new joy in your soul palate.

Make your way to a fertile new land. Put your roots down there. Reap a fruitful harvest. That your people too may know peace and no longer only imagine it. And, following the tenants of wellness, welcome heartfully all who come. For peace is a land that cannot be owned, bartered, or walled off. Peace is not a property. Peace is profoundly free.

LET YOUR LOVE GO FORTH to every soul you meet, saying *You are safe with me.*

Every soul is a hummingbird looking for a safe place to land. This world does not lack Love. It lacks Love encounters. Spaces where Love has been released to flow freely. Don't add to the drought. Add to the monsoon. First comes your Love. Then healing comes soon. First comes sunlight. Then the glory of the moon.

SHE MADE JOY her lifelong art project. Quickly, her art became priceless. To her. To everyone.

Some feel hopeless that they will ever achieve joy. Joy is not to be achieved. It is to be allowed. It is in us, waiting. First we choose to believe it is there. Then we do the work of allowing it to flow, gradually, patiently removing the inner barriers in the mind, heart, and body. Planting joyful thought and emotion habits.

Water joy's seed so it will release its sprout. Do not wait for your life to be right to be joyful. Be joyful and your life will be right. Joy is not a circumstance, a consequence of things going well for us. Joy is a way of being. A way we learn once we decide we want joy enough, and that we are tired enough of being joyless. Like all things, joy comes with practice. It is not exclusive to certain people. It is an energy arising from a determined art project: the lifelong jubilant crafting of your soul.

YOUR SOUL IS AS A GREAT WHALE. It takes you down into depths that can seem heavy. It breaches the surface for air. Sometimes it leaps, sunlight sparkling on its skin. It is a living thing. What you are feeling is its life. The life and moods and wanderings of your soul.

I LOVE MYSELF. Repeat these words until it no longer hurts to say them. Until they no longer feel false. Until they become your testimony. Your mantra. Your medicine. If the words feel foreign, give them time. They belong to you. They are your native song. At first, your heart is tender when you touch it in new ways. Keep touching. Your dear heart has knots and scars and adhesions. It wants to open and purr, though. So apply your daily ointment: *I Love myself*. Don't just moisturize your skin. Moisturize your heart. Soften your soil. This is how you care for the sovereign, sacred land that is your life.

I SIT IN THE GARDEN, in the poetry of blossoms, in the poetry of bees, butterflies, and hummingbirds, in the poetry of a swimming sun and the dance of fragrance, and I open and breathe poetry, and I write and read poetry. I harvest meaning from this life, for soon I will be the green ripening passion fruit on the vivacious vine. I scan the garden and note the array of colors and how they cannot be colors without their contrast, their outline of moods. The palm seeds drop heavy and drum the patient earth. A peace waves in my soul, like the Mexican feather grass surrounding me silently, like a music only the contented can bear to hear.

ONCE YOU DETERMINE not to let circumstance dictate your life, you go about Lovingly pulling yourself together, gathering all your pieces. Harvesting your wild fruit previously growing beyond where you allowed yourself. Peace is the greatest of these fruits, found only in the lush valley of wholeness. No matter how long or deep your suffering has been, no matter how far you have been scattered into pieces, you can live in peace. Faith is the walk. Truth is the harvesting tool. Your life is the wilderness. Let the gathering begin.

BELIEVE IN THE OLD MEDICINE WAYS. They allowed us to survive and thrive to reach these new days. Sacredness. Ceremony. Harmony with living things. Natural medicine. Rhythm and intimacy. Intuition and spirit. All our relations.

MANY PEOPLE ARE MORE COMFORTABLE with you in oppression than in freedom. Remember this when you face resistance. Discomfort them.

BE A GOOD HOST TO YOUR HAPPINESS. Make it feel welcome and invited. Be patient with its arrival. Encourage it to make itself at home. Send your unwanted guests on their way. Burn some sage. Clean up for your happiness. Open the windows and freshen the rooms. Prepare the little things. Leave Love notes on the pillows. Greet it warmly. Put on its favorite music. Ask what it is hungry for. Pour lots of tea. Ask about its family. All happiness has a family. Offer it your best bed and blankets. Ask what it wants to do today. Give it space. Don't rush it out the door. Invite it to stay anytime. Cherish its presence. Express your cherishing. Hug your happiness with all your heart.

YOU ARE OKAY, DEAR SOUL.

Every living thing aches as it changes.

One of the greatest challenges we have with change is the story that too often blooms in us. The one that says *I am not okay. The sky is falling. This fear and pain mean something is dreadfully wrong.*

Such stories of panic and despair amplify our pain and sense of aloneness. Practice reminding yourself that you are changing, and sometimes change feels like this. Keep your path in mind.

Sing soul songs like this: *I am a living, changing thing. Sometimes I ache. Sometimes I sing, together with every living thing. What treasure to travel this miracle road.*

And find new skies to lighten my load. Some mornings the sun shines on me. Some days I shine with epiphany.

Dear one, your body aches when you stretch it. So does your life.

TRY THIS ANCIENT REMEDY:

When you are tired, rest.

Blood Moon. Lunar eclipse. Mars nudging up on us. Whatever reason you need, grant yourself rest. Uproot the cultural guilt in you that says you have to be doing something. It is killing us. Choose life. All living things rest. Be a living thing.

We need your singular soul, not doing, just being. If you can learn to be at peace with your existence on its own, nothing added, you can taste freedom, wellness, and purpose at their peak ripeness. So many modern remedies for our exhaustion. One glaring ancient, proven medicine: May you bless your tenderness, your stress, and your heaviness with rest. Sweet, old-fashioned rest.

THINGS THAT WASH YOUR spirit clean: *Moonlight. Tears. Remembering yourself.* These are soul detergents. Life is a constant tide that can carry you out to sea, away from your true self. Have daily ceremonies that bring you back. Stay in your ceremonies. The ones that make you feel new, purified, clarified. What are your soul detergents?

YOU CANNOT FIND PEACE. It is not lost. It has always been in you. Set it free.

IF YOU CAN BELIEVE in your power to nurture more than you believe in your power to control, you will bless this world and not bruise it.

YOUR JOURNEY is a Love song of heartbeats and breaths. Cherish your tenderness.

EVERYONE HAS A LULLABY, lyrics by which they send themselves to sleep. Hopefully your lullaby is not a horror story. Maybe try a romantic comedy. Or a soothing documentary on the many traditions of peace.

ACTING IN SELF-LOVE is how you declare life. For everything. Acting against self-Love is how you declare war. Against everything. Declare life, you dear and precious river. Gush your soft, powerful being along its divine course. Feed every blossom in every valley and the resilient life on high mountain slopes. Feed the endless belly of sky and the living blanket of night. Feed all things, all ways, most of all your diaphanous, anointed soul. Make your offerings in morning's chorus of whispers, and all along sun's steady arc. Embark on inner kindness. Go forward, a bright, free rejoicing. Declare life.

WHAT IS YOUR ART? Today is your canvas for that.

THE WAY IS NOT AS HARD as your idea of the way. Let go of your idea and suddenly you are on your way.

ALL KINDS OF ANCESTORS roam our souls. You are becoming one. Live beautifully. You are creating the inheritance of so many souls to come. Behold how you touch this world. How you touch your life. Gather sacred plants: Kindness. Tenderness. Serenity. Love. Keep cleansing. Keep purifying. Keep breathing. Nurture yourself with every breath. Yes, that deeply. Now, deeper than that.

I AM JUST A BAKER. These words, my daily bread. I have one thing to offer: Love. We all have endless ways to serve this divine gift. All I am doing is sending this endless, aching river of Love through you. This Love is not mine, is not anyone's. It is a freedom flow.

YOU KNOW YOU ARE IN YOUR POWER when things don't happen to you. You happen to things.

Determine your life, dear soul. You are that powerful. Even more than you imagine. Always more. If you disbelieve in your power, you may not have glimpsed your power. For when you see the truth of it you cannot stop seeing it. We speak here of your power to make your life. To remake your life. For this, no boundaries or limits exist.

We do not run out of power. We run out of belief. Run back in. Tomorrow life is new. So, too, if you choose, are you. Be a happening. Experience the sensation of transformation. Imprint this canvas of life with your richest colors, your deepest hues of goodness. Goodness, look at you.

WE ARE ALWAYS LOOKING for some paradise water to wade out into. In any moment we can wade into the paradise of paradises: our own soul.

SOMETIMES, THE ONLY WAY onward is inward.

When you feel like you have exhausted every external option, maybe you are the answer you have been seeking. Maybe you are the medicine, the revelation, the illumination. Take a deep breath and turn to you. The real you, instinctive and intuitive and divine. You may be surprised how gifted you are at solving yourself. Surely you have a moment to spare for yourself. It may be the investment of a lifetime. Enjoy a wonderful journey.

I AM WORTHY. Wash your whole life in these words.

Self-Lovers stay in the water after everyone else has dried off. Soaked and saturated, they remain in a state of worthiness. If you ever find yourself wondering why a person would be kind to you, or whether you deserve to be happy and content, or reach your dreams, maybe you have been too long out of the water of self-Love and affirmation. It is never too late to wade back in. Look how sky washes itself. Be that devoted and thorough. And what are you worthy of? Everything good. Everything that is truly good.

YOU ARE QUALIFIED to bloom. Blooming is not only for flowers or springtime. You are qualified. Heal. Thrive. Don't just live. Be alive. You don't have to wait on more education, the right job, the perfect relationship, good weather, a specific astrological alignment, a good hair day, better seasoning in your food, being in better shape, more money, less stress, new shoes, easier opportunities, rainbows, full moons, friendship, a stronger back, weaker resistance, someone's permission, or anyone to understand you. Bloom now. Bloom now. Bloom now, you miraculous, unlimited alphabet of glory and mystery. Introduce us to your language of petals. Show us how you greet the merciful sun.

You are qualified to bloom. In every way. Give yourself permission. Release your lifetime of doubt, fear, and insecurity with a daily song: *I am qualified. I am worthy. I belong. I am a blossoming thing. I dance in sunlight. I arch my wings. I am kin to beautiful things. Never too late. Never too soon. Now, I bloom.*

YOU ARE NOT ONE of your people. You are all of them. Live in your power.

Some cultures sever themselves from their ancestral wealth, encouraging people to live as individuals insulated from their past, their kin, and their descendants. This delusional hyper-individualism breeds fear, insecurity, despair, loneliness, and careless relations with all living things.

Other cultures celebrate a daily life immersed in the richness of all their relations, including the very real spirit, Love, and presence of their ancestors. Souls who live in this way experience their individual selves as but a part of their acutely tangible collective selves, their relational oneness and intimacy with all things.

Existing in this way fosters deep inner peace, faith, calm, courage, compassion, duty, fruitfulness, and broader, deeper perspective. Our truer power derives not from a confused sense of individual potency, but from the epiphany that we are never alone, that we have no boundary of being, and that all things are possible in our life because we are in essence all things. You are the glory of this Creation. Not a grain of it. The glory of all of it. May you live in your power, dear soul. Ahó. Ashé. Amen.

KINDNESS DOES NOT BEGIN the moment you speak or act. It is the red carpet of Loving energy you roll out as you approach. It is your aura of invitation, your marquee announcing the safe space you are and the care you bring. Kindness begins with the healing work you do to purify your soul from the world's harm and pollution. It is a capacity to be open-hearted, to access your own affection. To move from closed self-concern to empathic attentiveness. Kindness breeds as a grace to which you treat yourself, then spreads like sky out from there. In a state of kindness, you are among the greatest of natural resources on earth. May you enjoy the immeasurable treasure of your own wealth of kindness.

IN THE DATING GAME of your emotional life, maybe you are ready to let anxiety know you feel it is time to start seeing other energies. Anxiety is a relationship, too. Just because that relationship may be years old, doesn't mean you should stay. Peace is always looking for new partners. Ones who speak its native language.

PEACE KNOWS YOUR ADDRESS. Make sure you are home. Be present within yourself. Move in. Open the windows. Let in the light. Freshen up the place. Make yourself a place you'd like to stay. Be a homebody.

SOME USE WORDS to obscure truth. Some use words to reveal truth. Filter it all through your soul. Discernment is everything. So are you when bathed in truth.

YOU AND PEACE go way back. Go ahead. Act like friends. If you don't remember how you and peace used to be, maybe it is because you have been giving fear and anxiety all your attention. Let peace know you would like to hang out like you used to. Peace is forgiving. It just wants your invitation. Open your heart. Release your tension. Have faith in your existence. In its sufficiency. Its validity. Open these doors. Peace will enter. Not from beyond you. From within you. Peace was with you all along.

BIG DIFFERENCE BETWEEN *Freedom here* and *Free dumb here*. You can get free dumb anywhere. Just because dumb is free doesn't mean you should pick some up. Get you some freedom.

WE DO NOT HAVE LONG to sing this song that is our holy life. Sing it. Sing it. Sing it. Don't wait. Here is your window of opportunity. Joy. Love. Laughter. Tears. Passion. Compassion. Creativity. Dreams. Dance. Daring. Gratitude. Exaltation. Vitality. Liberation. Testimony. These things matter. They enrich your life. They are your fire in the cold, in the dark. Light your fire.

MOONRISE. SUNRISE. SOULRISE. You are all of these. Behold yourself. What stirs you is stirred by you. Creation is a powerful reciprocity. Recognize what you are a part of. Feel it. It will wake in you and shine through you. Moon got you in a mood? You got moon in a mood, too. Know your power. Do good things with it. Your labor births you back to you.

YOU LOOK FOR LOVE in endless places, but Love is not in places. Love is a place. Look there. People. Animals. Locations. Jobs. Land. These things do not hold Love. Love is holding them. The place is not the thing. Love is the thing. Open to Love and you will have your place. Welcome home.

EAGLES DO NOT ASK for flight permission from wingless things.

Do the thing. They will tell you that you cannot do the thing. Let this denial be your doorway into doing the thing. Let their aversion and fear illuminate your purpose, path, and precious singularity.

Humanity around you may grasp at your wings to keep you from flight. Instead, use their energy for your wind. Kites don't care what the ground wants them to do. A song doesn't talk. It sings. You may see barriers and boundaries everywhere. Look again with new eyes. What you see are the peculiar invitations Love sometimes makes. When it comes to your purest callings, Love doesn't say *Don't*. Love always says *Do*.

EVERYTHING, WHETHER IT IS KIND or cruel to you, is showing you the way home to you. Look into the kindness and see your true nature and purpose. Look into the cruelty and see the consequence of being lost in pain's wilderness. Look into every soul. Every day. See yourself in new light.

PAIN DOES NOT MEAN you are weak. It means you are powerful. Pain is your power fighting to get out.

SOME WOULD LAND in another people's world and say *Take me to your paradise*. Others would land in another people's world and say *Take me to your pain*. Paradise may often be appealing and healing. Yet some souls cannot escape their compassion flame inside that always tilts toward touching pain with mercy's medicine. These empathic souls are healers. You may be one of them.

WORRY NOT SO MUCH ABOUT your fantasy wedding. Marry divine Love and every moment will be your perfect matrimony. Your other relationships will follow.

WHAT A PRIVILEGE IT IS TO BE YOU. Cherish your miraculous life. You are the one and only. Be fascinated with your experience. It is unrepeatable. Rejoice in that.

WHEN YOU FIGHT FOR FREEDOM, your entire soul is required. Let's start a revolution. Lovers over haters. Life over the living dead.

YOUR FACE IS POWERFUL. Be mindful of your expression. Your face can be a battering ram, a bullying weapon, a sharp knife for cutting. Or it can be an act of Love, a deep kindness, an invitation to safety, a healing gift. Your expression can determine your day, your life, and the world. Give good face.

SPEAKING AGAINST INJUSTICE is not divisive. Injustice is divisive. Always remember this. Some will try to silence you by accusing your expression against injustice and oppression as being a cause of conflict and hatred. But injustice and oppression are the cause of conflict and hatred. Always be suspicious of those who don't want you to address injustice. They don't want justice and they don't want peace and harmony. They want the status quo. They want the continuation of their comfort. They want Change itself to retreat, succumb, and surrender. Speak your truth. Stay free.

WHEN THEY ASK WHAT YOU DO for a living, say *I Love*.

If you aren't Loving, you aren't living. Whatever your profession, do not mistake your true vocation. Love. Not possession or control. Not having or wanting. A cherishing that sets all things free. An opening, not a closing. Softening, not hardening. Feeling the essence of a thing and letting that essence move through you in honor, wonder, gratefulness. Letting your essence flow freely outward. Sacred union. Here's to your life, which is your Love.

I LOVE YOU shouldn't be the hardest thing for you to say to yourself. The old tenderness in you needs a new language. Recruit new words. They will bring new feelings. You will have new life.

DON'T BE AFRAID to be the mystical creature you are. Be a *unique-corn*. They will never fully believe the true you actually exists anyway. Be the myth. Be the impossible. Be the inexplicable legend they seek in dreams. Give yourself this gift. Dissolve even your own idea of you. Freedom and peace bloom when you live. As. You. Are.

DO NOT MISTAKE THE BEAUTY of a Lover's body for the beauty of a Lover's soul. No matter how beautiful, you do not live with the body nearly as deeply as you live with the soul. Your Lover's soul will be your most consequential companion. Consider this.

SELF-LOVE SEES CLEARLY. Honors the truth. Weaves in ceremony with the communal self. Chooses bravely. Breathes beautifully. Always comes home.

KNOW THIS: If you dare follow your calling, your soul stirring, your fire, that divine urgency will drag you from your cave of fear out into the bravest light.

SPEAK YOUR DEAR TRUTH. Bless your life. And your generations. Your truth wakes all truth inside the truth of every soul. Dare to light that fire. Your truth is more sacred than their fear. Honor your truth.

DON'T JUST TAKE A BREATH for you. Take one for all of Creation. Breathe in a collective way. You will receive collective benefits. Symbiosis.

YOUR ANCESTORS SHED oceans of tears. You were the hope glistening in every single one. Know your legacy, and you know your worth. Know your worth, and you have the will to be free. Go now, sing your freedom songs.

FIRST, THEY IGNORE YOU. Then they laugh at you. Then they rage against your increasing influence. Finally, when your sacred offering becomes popular, they want to join you and claim they were your greatest champion all along. Stay as rooted in your true spirit as you were when they ignored you. Do not be seduced into being the fleeting centerpiece of their fickle celebration. Your calling itself cherishes you most.

HURT CAN BE THE HOPEFUL ACT of your soul reaching for its beautiful life. Breathe. Be ever so still and close with yourself. Then look closely at what you feel. It is a true friend pointing in the glorious direction of where you need to go.

IF YOU ATTEND YOUR SOUL the way you do your social world, you will have at least one true follower. Its name shall be Peace. Soul is an orchard of endless fruit, each ripe with the same sugar. The sugar of Peace.

YOU ARE WORTHY. Worthy. Worthy of what? A beautiful life. Healing. Honor. Hope. Courage. Release. Respect. Peace. Poetry. Passion. Calm. Stability. Solitude. Safety. Love. Relationship. Forgiveness. Forgiving. Joy. Laughter. Belonging. Appreciation. Affection. Celebration. Fruitfulness. Abundance. Cherishing. Sensuality. Freedom. Liberation. Achievement. Rest. Restoration. Renewal. Voice. Choice.

Leadership. Humility. Grace. Glory. Goodness. Growth. Wisdom. Wildness. Wellness. Truth. Transformation. Inspiration. Brilliance. Creativity. Kindness. Compassion. Revolution. Song. Service. Singularity. Sacredness. Dance. Ceremony. Prayer. Revival. New life. New life. New life.

BE PATIENT WITH THE POETRY that is your life. If you Love the wine, be patient with the grape. If you Love peace, be patient with your soul. It is a ripening thing. If you Love joy, be patient with your life. It is a sweetening thing. Patience is how you optimize the orchard of your existence.

YOU NEED NOT WORRY about knowing yourself. Spend time with yourself. Knowing will come. When you spend time with your soul, fully present, caring, feeling, laughing, listening, seeing, realizing, releasing, exploring, learning, and Loving, you will come to know your soul. Have faith in your ability to know. You cannot worry yourself into knowing. But you can be present, which births knowing. Self-knowing is a plant that grows and blooms with care. Its sun, soil, air, and water are in you. You release them by being with you. Be the party, adventure, action, destination, location, person, crowd, event, sanctuary, serenity you most want to spend time with tonight. Tomorrow. In your days to come.

YOU CANNOT PUNISH a person into healing and growth. Only Love can do that. Punishment can create superficial change but not inspired transformation of the soul. Only Love can do that. Punishing others is seductive and appeals to our ego. Only Love appeals to the other's soul.

To this day, our institutions and ways are fear, control, and punishment-based. Our children complete their education with incomplete personas, having been damaged by years of punishment and fear flooding their brains and bodies in the form of inflammatory, destructive cortisol, adrenaline, and self-punishing thoughts. They may graduate, but from what? Punishment school? As what? Master punishers? Into what? The punishment factory of the adult world?

Our workplaces are saturated with fear and punishment-based energy and culture. As a result, our adults are the walking dead. Exhausted, traumatized carriers of a lifetime of fear and punishment. Giftedness, passion, vision, freedom, courage, creativity, light, and joy leached from their breath and bones. Do we wish to be caught forever in a cycle of fear and punishment? Or do we care to taste the sublime freedom of wellness, peace, and wholeness? Only Love can do that.

Love is the supreme instrument of musical ecstasy. Love is where sacred dancing and singing happen. What if we train ourselves to be a culture of Lovers? There is a gym for that: The heart. This gym is open 24 hours, shows up wherever you do, and has every piece of equipment you need, perfectly designed and calibrated for you. And you don't have to wait in line for your turn.

Love has a way of getting the attention of our molecules and cells. Love says to them *Leap into me. I make all things new.* They do. Leap. If we want more pain and suffering, we always have punishment. It seems so promising in the eyes of our vengeance. It can create mass remorse but not intimate renewal. As for our homes, programs, and systems, when a care house becomes a warehouse, all is lost. If we want healing and peace, only Love, true life, can do that.

WHATEVER YOUR HEART is feeling, rub some Love on it. Self-medicate in a sacred way.

EVERYONE WANTS EVERYONE'S ATTENTION. Attend your soul. You will have your perfect attention.

SOLITUDE CAN SAVE YOUR SANITY. If you socialize with it.

MENTAL ILLNESS is when your soul suffers as it revolts against a sick worldly reality. Mental wellness is when your soul wins the revolution.

YOUR BODY IS A SACRED LAND. Your heart is a sacred land. Your dreams are a sacred land. Treat what is sacred sacredly and you will have new life.

BE ENCOURAGED. Everywhere you go, Love is. You are always home.

REMEMBER. You are moon-like. Swayer of tides.

YOU WERE FORMED from your ancestors' tears. You have enough Love in you to water your own life. The idea that we are each an individual, separate from all things, creates more loneliness, destruction, and helplessness than any other idea. It is a false idea from a suffering culture and not true to how most cultures have always existed.

All your people's goodness before your time is concentrated in you. To release this sacred water, all you need to do is believe this. You are the continuation of a mighty river. Not alone or impotent in life. Entirely immersed in the company of All Things. Potent beyond your dreams. Remember your true self. You are a strand of sweetgrass in the sacred braid of life. If you Love anything in this world, then what you are Loving *is* yourself. Recognize the rest of you. Release your broken way of seeing you. Everywhere you gaze in Love you gaze the Love you are.

LOVE IN YOU has never been hurt, cannot be touched. Is immortal. Infinite. Immeasurable. Is a fountain yearning to spill over, everywhere you go.

BOW LIKE SUNLIGHT to the flower that is your soul. It will blossom for you. Learn to be a flowering thing and your whole life can be a garden. Paradise lives inside you. Be your favorite destination.

WE DO NOT LIVE a beautiful life because we happen to find beauty, but because we choose to be beautiful. You, my friend, are a living field of the most divine flowers. You have no need to wait on someone to buy you a rose.

LIFE HAS LEARNED A NEW Love song. You are its notes. Introduce us.

YOUR SOUL IS AN INFINITE OCEAN. That's why your tears taste like sea. Tears are evidence of the soul, and how your soul purifies itself. Let them come. Bathe tonight in your own soul water. Tears of gratitude and release taste like sugar to the appetite that is your life.

FREEDOM ISN'T SOMETHING you gain from the world. It is something you raise inside yourself.

WITHOUT CEREMONY, how can your gathering have a clear purpose and context? Without clear purpose and context, a gathering becomes a scattering of random seeds, easily lost to the wind of life. With ceremony, a gathering exudes sacredness. Stories come alive with intent and determined spirit. Gather in a sacred way.

IF YOU GIVE ME YOUR STORIES and languages, and I give you my tokens and promises, I will have your power and life, and you will have my bribe. Do not fall for being colonized. Do not sign treaties drafted by sickened souls and cultures. It is a bad bet. An even worse life plan. And the worst possible investment in your generations. Keep your stories and languages. Reject tokens and promises. Make a treaty with your soul. Never break it.

WHAT YOUR BODY DOES in prayer does not matter as much as what your heart and soul are doing. Eyes closed. Eyes open. Kneeling. Dancing. Crying. Laughing. Loud. Silent. As long as your heart and soul are gushing with Love's sanctity, with Sovereign water, all of this is prayer.

THE RUMORS ARE TRUE. Life Loves you. You are alive. This means sky is Loving you. Earth is Loving you. All of Creation is feeding, watering, nurturing, caring for, and healing you. Life Loves you. It looks after you, considers you, forgives you, sustains you. Life is inspired by you.

You watch flowers bloom. Flowers do the same to you. Do not question your Love-worthiness. Love for you is not a mythical unknown, is more than a whisper. Each day, you have your abundant evidence all around and within you. May you know peace in this. And when you wonder, may you find your way back to the truth. Your proof is profound. You are Loved.

IF YOU DO NOT SWIM DAILY in the river of your truth, you are soon swept out to a fateful sea. Sow the seeds of your own stories. Be earth for your generations.

BELOVED, YOUR LIFE is happening now. Don't be late. Enough planning, hoping, dreaming, waiting, wanting. Here is your miraculous life. It offers itself to you in every moment, with every breath. Take it. It is yours. It always was.

YOUR ANCESTORS HAVE SO MUCH faith in you, they keep planting their dreams in your heart. If you are going to follow anything, follow your dreams. They are soaked in ancestral Love and lead you to the legend of your life.

SHE CURLED UP by the fire of her Love for herself. All aspects of herself including other living things. It was the warmest, most peaceful night of her life.

THE BRAVEST SOULS are brave enough to Love. Not just to Love those like them. All living things. Love is a gift to the self. A fire for the cold in your own soul. Like a sacred thread, it mends the fabric of this world we depend on to live a beautiful life.

SUMMON THE WILL to face the terrible, so you may birth the beautiful.

IF YOU WANT GOOD YAM (life), prepare good soil (soul).

ALL THE DAYS IN BETWEEN your birthdays. Let those be your celebration. Celebrate for 364 days, so that on the 365th, you may savor a year of being all the way alive.

IT IS POSSIBLE to be so absolutely bursting with Love that your soul has no room for hate. You are that divine fruit. Keep ripening.

PARADISE IS NOT A PLACE. It is a condition of the heart. Some travel to all the world's wondrous places and never truly arrive, for they go with a clenched heart that binds them to the shadowed muting of their usual life. Others stay home yet arrive over and again to the most enchanting places and discoveries. For they live with a wide open heart that journeys ever beyond the body as a spirit in Love with life. Open your phenomenal heart. Travel beautifully.

YOU ARE THE ABSOLUTE embodiment of your ancestor's deepest Love, dreams, prayers, hopes, pain, and healing. Treat yourself sacredly. The value of your life has grown through generations of souls yearning for one who would come and fulfill what they did not. When you are down on yourself, remember this. You are their best chance for freedom. This is not a burden. It is an open sky of possibility. You are not the sum of your suffering. You are the boundlessness of infinite beauty.

WE GLORIFY MOON for its shine, when it is sun that gives us moonlight. Be sun to the moons in your life. Be that kind of uncredited light.

REPRESENTATION MEANS everything to people who do not have it. Those who have always placed themselves at the center of every story wonder what the big deal is. Having not known the cold desolation at the margins, they are swollen with false self-importance. Fill your life and your world with the goodness of your own truth. To those at the margins we say *Grow used to being at the center*. To those who have hoarded the center we say *Your oppressing ways destine you for the margins of a healing world. Where we pray you will grow humility's medicine in your heart.*

WHAT YOU MAY CALL cause for loneliness, call reason for joy. Solitude throws a party, invites everyone. Few arrive. You can. Stay all night feasting endlessly.

YOU DON'T HAVE ANXIETY. Anxiety has you. Anxiety has you fooled and addicted. It isn't easy to give it up. You will need to heal it out of you, this narcotic that is everywhere. Consider that your culture itself is anxious. To heal from your anxiety, you may need to acknowledge that it is not your anxiety. It is everyone's. When the air is dirty, you don't say *I have dirty air*. You say *The air is dirty*. Your culture is anxious. You may need broader measures to heal anxiety in you. Such as living an uncommon, ancestrally rooted life. So you may be medicine for our collective calm.

THEY WANT YOU TO BE ASHAMED of your name, skin, hair, features, history, stories, and culture. Love these territories. They are your sovereign land. Love cherishes itself. This is how it stays free.

YOU AREN'T THE FRUIT to be picked. You are the orchard. Live abundantly. You are the earth. Water. Wind. Sun. Seeds. Roots. Living whole is an art when your kind has been taught to live in parts. Bless you. You are forever ripening. Endlessly abundant. You have no need to treat yourself as an offering for other people's appetites. May your own appetite find its greatest satisfaction in your plenitude. Your irrevocable personhood. You are the source, not the serving. If you live as an orchard, those who come to walk your earth will do so sacredly. You are worthy of this kind of Love.

HAY COSAS QUE IMPORTAN y cosas que no. Cuidé sagradamente.

There are things that matter and things that don't. Care sacredly.

Care, not just in crisis. Also in calm. Calm is that soil where we plant the seeds of endurance, resilience, healing, and social communion, that they may bloom in crisis and bring us wholly (holy) back to calm. Send this Love medicine for suffering everywhere in this Creation.

HUMAN KIND OR HUMAN CRUEL. We must decide. And then we must commence the ultimate revolution. If we do not weave our sacred basket (the world) with care, kindness, and Love, it cannot hold sacred water (life). This is the everlasting truth of things.

A reckoning is upon us. As our Indigenous ancestors teach us, two wolves are fighting in every soul. The wolf of Love and the wolf of hate. Only one can win, though they will forever fight until dominance is established in the personal and collective soul. For this is the way of wolves. Which one will win in you? The one you feed the most. Which one will win in us? The one we feed the most. This is a sacred teaching. Its deeper meaning must come to us through sacred ceremonies and teachers.

Too many souls are feeding the wolf of hate. Thus, fires of suffering are blistering our world. We call out now for healers. Are you one? Claim it so. Announce yourself. Offer your life to this struggle upon us. Now is the time for truth no matter how hard. Now is the season of sacred gathering and sacred storytelling. We must learn to feed each other again.

Let us gather in the valleys, on the mountains, by the sea, in the desert and forest, and on the plains. Let us bring our grain and pollen. Ocean seeping from our eyes, let us suffer tenderly together and rise on laughter into remembering ourselves. This, dear one, is not a time for soullessness and selfish wandering. It is a season to enter the sacred circle, the holy hoop, to dance and sing and cleanse our souls in cedar smoke.

We have inherited old sickness. We yearn for new wellness, which is itself older than our sickness. Someone go back to the beginning and bring us purity. Paint us with that wild berry medicine. Sky waits for us to be beautiful on earth. Take a deep breath, kindred ones, and be ready to shed this outgrown and sullen human coat.

Bright sun speaks to us a blessing. Let us hold each other and feed our wolf of Love.

WE CALL OUT NOW for healers. Are you one? *Por favor*, announce yourself. A new way isn't coming. A new way is here. Fear-rooted violence and conquest culture is out of fashion. Its weakness and toxicity have been exposed. Going forward, we need healers to move to the front. Please, raise your hand. Your time is here. Breathe through your fears. Share with us your ancestral power.

WHEN YOU FEEL LESS THAN beautiful, remember. You are the beadwork adorning your ancestors. When you feel unable, remember. You are Ancestor-powered. For those who hold their ancestors close and dear, you drink from a mighty river, stand on a majestic mountain, eat from fertile plains of harvest, and are warmed in a sacred blanket of sky. Your power is not individual. It is the song and surging of all things. You have been Loved for thousands of years. Remember who you are.

STILL HERE. As you move through, anticipating suffering, experiencing suffering, and healing from suffering, two words are your reminder, affirmation, and lantern on the forward road: *Still here*. I am still here.

LEARN IN A THOUSAND LANGUAGES to say *I Love you*, to your soul. Your soul is a plant you cannot overwater with Love. Water your soul in every moment. Drench it all the way to beautiful. Flush out the generations of pain and false identity. Wash your life back to life. Let Love be that soul water.

HOW DO YOU KNOW you are healing? When your pain, which once felt like the whole sky, starts to feel like a cloud, and you, who once felt like a small cloud, start to feel like the whole sky.

WHEN LIFE GROWS HARD, soften. Become water-like, so you may flow through it all and come out purified.

I LOVE YOU. I cherish you. I appreciate you. With these words, you can change the world. Apply this medicine to every soul you meet, including your own. Repeated applications may be necessary.

YOU DESERVE A BIG, beautiful, Loving breath. Go ahead, gift your whole life. With life. I wish you beautiful breathing. It infuses everything with energy, healing, calm, and renewal. Enjoy a spa with no cost. Soak yourself in a luxurious, relaxing bath of breathing. Stay there.

FEELING DEEPLY doesn't require that you suffer. You can be an empath with an ocean inside and still soothe your heart with gentle song. You can cradle the world's pain and tenderness in a sacred basket of Loving kindness. Let your feelings float like feathers. Sweet talk the heaviness into breeze. Lullaby your heavenly heart. So it can dream you all the way to peace.

LOVE AND YOU go on a date. You ask *Do you think we will last forever?* Love answers *Dear soul, we* ARE *forever.*

THE ANSWER FOR EVERYTHING: *Make Love.* Those who do not know how to make divine Love in this world are as people in a cold wilderness who do not know how to make fire. Sacred artists make Love from every moment, every encounter. Love songs, sculptures, dances, murals. Kindness is a Love creation. Where you find pain, paint your Love on that porous wall. Love is what we are here for. If you are not making Love, what are you making?

THE SHORE IS CLOSER than it looks. Even the rough water carries you there. I know you are tired. Keep rowing.

YOU HAVE THE RIGHT to remain in your true voice. What you don't say, can and will be used against you in a court of freedom. You have the right to an ancestor. You can always afford one, so one need not be appointed to you. Do you understand these rights?

SHE OPENED THE NOTE she retrieved from the buried box beneath the willow tree. Tears flowed over her smile as she read the words she had written as a little girl: *I am going to be a woman who is a safe place for herself.*

LOVE DOES NOT CONTAIN obligations. It only contains Love. Live in your Love today. It is sufficient and full of Grace.

LIKE WIND SHAPING COASTAL TREES, pain contorts each soul uniquely. And, if you let it, with a kind of beauty so singular and incomprehensible, it can only be divine.

COME CLOSER, let me whisper a secret to happiness: *Be in Love with everything.*

Love is an ecstasy worth the dare. Strip naked of your reasons not to Love. Go bare out into the world and be enamored by every wonder. It is all a wonder and we are starving to be enchanted.

YOU DON'T HAVE TO MOVE THROUGH challenges in heaviness and hardness. You can choose lightness and ease and still reach the other side. We learn how to deal with life from many people who themselves don't know the most healthful ways of dealing with life. Generational suffering habits and suffering addictions. It is not true that with difficult moments we must extract all possible suffering from the difficulty. We have the right and the ability to take flight and move like feather clouds through our moments of challenge. No need to feel guilty about being at peace and easy on yourself. You deserve to get through it and nurture yourself all along the way.

THE TEA YOU POUR should be the tea you drink. Take care that when you discover an idea, you don't fall into it and drown. Stay free. Ideas are not truth. Truth is truth. Burn sage all you want, but what are you really burning? Is your soul aflame? Are you clearing your space, cleansing your spirit, or only polluting your life with ritual that does not touch your depths? What do you see swimming at the surface? Is it the sky or is it a fantasy of fear and safety? Bless what you see. Bless what you touch. Bless all that is exposed to you. Take care like this.

IF A CHILD HANDS YOU a flower, then asks for the flower back, do you suffer? If you do not suffer, why? If you do suffer, why? It is good to be in touch with the meaning we give to sharing, receiving, and giving. Peace and wellness are at stake.

ALL THAT YOU ARE is sacred. You don't have to acquire sacredness. You just have to remember yourself. Sacredness. That you may live in a good way. So you may be medicine for the world. And all your relations, all living things, may dance a ceremony of gratitude for your spirit and its beauty offerings in this world.

REST EASY, DEAR ONE. Your life Loves you.

TO BREATHE or not to breathe. That is the question. The beginning and end of all peace and anxiety are rooted in how we breathe. If your lungs are compromised, breathe with your entire soul. Breathe with your entire soul regardless. Breathe with your whole body, every cell. Breathe your wounds into wellness.

Marry your Love to your breath, and be a freedom dancer sending them both out to touch souls, a bouquet of kindness. Breathe hope into your bones. Recruit sky, sun, moon, and breathe with them, too. Breathe with all the oceans, all the lands, and all your ancestors.

Breathe to give your people breath, for we are in a poverty of breathing. Breathing is a candle illuminating this world. A wild herb tea with great healing powers the old ones used to gather daily. Breathing is a shepherd leading its flock to peace. You are a holy ceremony when you breathe.

YOUR PHENOMENAL SOUL cannot be understood. You are not here for that. You, like all phenomena, are here to be experienced. Be at peace with that. Sacred one, spend your life being you, not explaining you. We need the light of your truth even as we do not fully comprehend it. You need the peace of being secure in your truth. So it may be fulfilled. *Osiyo*. It is good in you.

MAY IT BE SAID that in your time, you brought Love into the world. Stop all your practices except Love. Lose yourself in that ultimate art.

A THOUSAND RIVERS live in you, each an ancestor singing an ancient song. Each day, go down to the river. Listen closely. Come back to your life drenched and soaking in the sacred sound.

THE WAY THE SUN FEELS on your skin after a cold night. Arrive like that to every soul. Your aura is your legacy. Be a better ancestor today. May we be deeply caring with the energy we exude. In many ways, it is more powerful than the sun, lasts longer than fossils, births the spirit of our clan, community, and nation, and affects the weather inside endless souls. What we need most in the world are Lovers. If you are one, your legend will be told forever.

THIS LOVE THING you are here for, erase all your ideas and let it come.

LYING ON A BRIGHT MEADOW, you find such peace in the blue sky. Awaken that sky inside your soul.

IF YOU HAVE MADE A MESS, congratulations. You have just taken the first step in making a masterpiece. Is your life a mess? Then it is on its way to being a masterpiece. Hopefulness is not a fortune born of circumstance. It is a chosen habit, a way of seeing. An embrace of untidy imperfection. May you be hopeful today, wherever you are in your immensely divine journey.

THE GREATEST WORK you can do in this world is inside you. Do you wish to change the world? Change your inner condition. Do you wish to change the culture? Change your ways. Want a healthier society? Change your mind. Yearn to serve lives? Serve the life you are living. Care to heal human suffering? Heal your suffering, human. World peace? Peace your inner world. Want to be an activist? Activate your compassion. Clean the oceans? Clean the ocean that is your soul. Climate change? Change your spiritual climate. And if you want more kindness, learn to honor the singular kind you are.

LOVE IS A VAST LANDSCAPE everyone talks about visiting. Few are willing to cross into it and stay forever.

BE A TUNER OF SOULS. Love's music is waiting.

IT WAS ALWAYS YOU. You are the library where you should lose yourself. The book you should read. The language you should learn. The place you should voyage. The discovery you should make. All the world's wonder is a song. The notes and the singer are you.

IF YOU HURT, maybe you are sprouting from the hard seed shell. Or breaking up through the crust. Or stretching into stalk. Or birthing branches. Or blossoms. Or fruit. Maybe you are the glory of a growing thing. And surely good.

LOVE'S GREATEST EVIDENCE is kindness. To behold your self-Love journey, notice your growing of self-kindness, and the way it spreads itself out from you to encompass other living things. Your kindness is an introvert and an extrovert. Let it follow its river of moods.

EXPLAINING YOUR OWN MYSTIC SOUL to anyone is like trying to bring the ocean onto shore in one mouthful. Be at peace with the ocean you are. The right ones will join you in the water.

IF YOU COULD FEEL what every living thing is feeling, you would be so in Love with life, you would never stop crying joy. Go ahead. Feel it.

HOPE IS THE LIGHT bursting forth from the story you tell yourself. Despair is what remains when your story chases all the light away. Mend your story. Your peace ability blooms when you realize it is your story, not your circumstance that ultimately makes your life.

SELF-LOVE ISN'T ONLY about Loving yourself. It's about Loving the world, and all that is, has been, and will be. Finding that inside you. Seeing yourself as the fine touches on a generational, patient, persistent, masterpiece of art. An all-inclusive Love affair.

ALL YOUR LIFE, what you thought was your voice was the voices of your ancestors filtered through your soul. They are the groundwater you have been drinking from the spring of your spirit. They wove the breeze that blankets you. Even the way you dance and sing is an old rhythm you are only bringing back into style.

This is not to say you are not original and do not have sovereign will. We are saying that you are not alone. You never have been and never will be. Your power is not the power of a person. This is a lie your oppressors planted in you. Your power is a power of ages, a rich milk of millennia, a stew seasoned to nourish your soul labor. Your elders went out to gather food in the forest. In each moment of your life, they offer this food and its force to you.

BE YOUR FAVORITE LIVING THING. You have the right to Love yourself this much. It is your duty to your soul. Peace begins with cherishing what you already are. So you can experience this world joyfully, without anxious wanting. Long night. Short day. Full belly moon. Peace be with you.

HOW CAN A BUTTERFLY do butterfly things if it has no sky? Grant the people in your relationships their own sky. Space and freedom can bring out the best in a soul, and spark harmony inside our intimacy.

LET US CEASE CALLING PEOPLE *influencers*. It is elitist language that once again reduces the masses and fortifies human caste systems. Of course, every living thing has influence. We have such a hard time being free. Don't we?

LET US DEVOTE OURSELVES to the freedom of living things. Love's freedom. Freedom to be true. Freedom to heal, change, grow. To fulfill calling and purpose and to live in giftedness. Freedom from oppression and the tyranny and terrorism of hate and supremacy. Freedom to release. To receive. To not conform. Freedom to learn, to language. To be. To remember. To belong and feel beautiful. To be dearly understood, affirmed, cherished, celebrated, honored. Especially by yourself. Freedom to exist a wild and living thing.

IF YOU ARE GOING TO HAVE offspring, may one of them be inner peace. Birth and raise beautiful things.

YOUR SOUL IS BEAUTIFUL. Make peace with that. Go, and make some peace with that.

ALWAYS PAUSE FOR POETRY. Everything is poetry.

YOU SEE? You made it through. Remember this the next time.

YOUR SOUL IS THE SOUL OF THE WORLD poured into a person. Revel in your abundance and beauty.

AND LOVE SAID *Take a deep breath, human flower. Now I am going to open you the rest of the way.*

HERE'S THE THING. Freedom does not ring if it is not for everyone.

SILENCE IS A SACRED CLASSROOM where all your best teachers are waiting for you. All inspiration needs is a crack in your noise-habit to let its light river through. Better yet, open all your windows and bathe in quietude. Peace is an eager dove waiting outside the glass.

LOVE IS NOT A FRUIT you reach to pick. It is a divine air in you and all around you. No more reaching. What you want, you already are. Breathe. You're all good. Literally. You are all that is good.

SAYING OR WRITING more words is not always a sign of intelligence. Silence can be genius. Closely examine its vocabulary. The purpose of expression is to share truth, not to impress. Impressions fade like sand prints in the wind. Truth cleanses. Heals. Sometimes, words. Sometimes, the song of silence.

SOUL IS AN OCEAN made for giving and receiving, for absorbing and reflecting, for starlight and sunlight. What falls into it surrenders and drowns eventually, only to be blessed back into birth as coral and creatures of depth and singing. Your soul-mist stains sky, which then rains back down its delight. Soul is ocean, is sky, is the way you dance through your living, and in living, surrender to the divine dance.

ALL THIS TALK of the prime of your life. The prime season of your life is when you are alive.

THE LANDS BETWEEN your *painfalls* are fertile earth eager to bear new life. Tend them.

ALL LIVING THINGS, even the breeze, are intoxicated on life in the wake of rain. You smell the scent of all that has lived and died and is birthing again. The hips of life widen as hope gathers in the birth canal. The vaginal *Sipapu* (Hopi), the place of emergence, dilates like sky at dawn.

Oh how the ancestors moan as the rivers cramp and the mountains ache, a contraction of the Land pounding like a drum, tearing through like lightning. Energy gathers itself in great heaps and tides. The order of things tightens and unravels at once. Miracles emerge through the pain. Everything is crying. Grief applauds its own performance. Loud, silent clapping from the molecules and elements. An orchestra of grief plays earth-culture classics and original dream music spawned and spermed and egged from the Love-making chemistry of clay and clouds.

Can you smell it now? The scent of breaching? The pungency of revival after the flood? Just last moment you were weeping and afraid. The mystery had no name, so you called it *Crisis*. But the mystery peeled away all you thought was real. Lies bloomed everywhere in that vacancy, like an invasive species. Now that you can see them, the lies, you realize they were there all along. They were your inherited and forged belief system.

Now, that sand castle is dying. You thought you were superior somehow. The flood killed your castles and overcame your moats. Left you naked and homeless. Vulnerable to the night and cold. All your accolades meant nothing. Your categories laughed at themselves before crying themselves to death. Who were you without your attachments? Your order and delusion of safety?

A virus killed your society. Killed its facade. Translated its propaganda into the language of fear and arrogance, greed and corruption. So much dirt in your laundry. So much sewage in your social sanctuary. Forlorn, you sought comfort and companionship. But the virus ran through your web, destroying your connections. You felt alone in the wind, a solitary thread bobbing and blameless on the tattered edge of what had been your web of life, your way of being.

Pollinators came for your flowering lies. They brought an amber manna of truth. We are all praying now. That you accept the manna and make it your majesty. That you gather the clay and the rain and the stain and the pain, and with your bare hands and on your bare knees, you bellow and bawl at the sky while you fashion of your soul a new vessel. An instrument fit for the music musicians manifest when they want something, anything, to heal.

JUST BECAUSE STORIES get passed around in a family and through its generations until they are held as gospel truth does not mean those stories are true. Negative, slandering, or dehumanizing stories are to varying degrees a volatile cocktail of imagination, projection, hearsay, fear, insecurity, trauma, rumor, gossip, spite, misinterpretation, misunderstanding, missing context, oppression-motive, deceit, manipulation, justifying, guilt reduction, time-worn mutation and distortion, and actual lived experience.

Each of us is bathed in these stories throughout our childhood, and arrive into adulthood with a certainty about them, an emotional identity attachment to what we have always believed. To be free souls and not slaves, we must be willing to examine and question our beliefs. Daily. For the rest of our lives.

TONIGHT, PUT ON MUSIC that melts you. Slow dance with your own soul. Do you wish to be free? Gather all the stories planted in your soil (soul) over your lifetime and burn them in a ceremonial fire. What turns to ash and disappears in the sky were never your sacred stories to begin with. What turns to ash, feeds the earth of your healing life, and reemerges to flower in your now conscious heart and Loving discernment, those are your sacred stories. Carry them with you. Water them well. Sing to them. Send them far. If they are sacred, they will find the souls who need them, to nourish them, so they, too, can be free.

THINGS HAVE CHANGED since yesterday. Hallelujah. For this is life.

EVERY NIGHT, you take refuge in your home. Refuge from the cold, the dark, the danger. You take refuge in your clothes, your car, your companions. You take refuge in your job, your paycheck, your groceries, and graces. Each day, you take refuge in your prayers, your faith, your community, and habits and rituals. You take refuge in your identity, your beliefs, your memories, and hopes. By the moment, you take refuge in your next breath and heartbeat. In your stay from death and in your lakes of emotion.

You take refuge in every minute fragment of your life. You are a refugee. You have always been a refugee. You will always be a refugee. Open your heart. Have compassion and show mercy for every refugee in this Intricately vulnerable, so often terrifying, feverishly inhospitable world.

ONE OF THE LAST THINGS we are willing to give up is our idea of who we think we are. Even as this idea is littered, polluted, poisoned with and distorted by thoughts, feelings, experiences, inherited stories, pain and trauma, misunderstandings, and so much more that is not innate or intrinsic to our soul.

Our beliefs, while at times helpful or beneficial in a certain moment of our life, can be a prison at least as easily as they can be a means of survival or thriving. If we are willing to breathe deeply and wade bravely into the waters of examining our self-idea, we can begin a journey whose very nature and soul rewards are an ephemeral condition we can fairly call *Freedom*.

THINGS ARE STIRRING tonight. Ocean wants to make Love with the moon. Can you feel their passion in you? Maybe you will join them in their great, aching bath of ecstasy. Maybe you will lose your composure and dissolve in the darkness, become the moon-blush on leaves. Maybe you will spill all your saltwater and crumble to your knees. Things are stirring tonight. Maybe you are one of them.

EVERYONE IS IN THE TAVERN drinking impotent brew. Stay out in the empty street dancing in the moonlight. Tomorrow you won't be hung over, and a thousand rivers of inspiration will run through you. Find your *soulship* with the mystics of all species. They will light a joy-fire in your heart. Communion with them daily. Die together with laughter. Let the Love wine pour endlessly. All the vagrant, delinquent poets will join you and fill your cup tremendously. Everyone will walk everyone home safely before dawn.

PLACE THE SORROW of your present season on the windowsill like a candle. Let the breeze have its fair chance to stroke the flame as your sorrow-candle needs. When it is time, the breeze can gently blow out the flame.

MAY I SHOW YOU something? Here, sit with me by this stream. Now, let's listen for a while. Hear that? Not the water. The way your heart sighs at the water's song. Hear that. Learn the music of your heart sighing. Feed it the songs it hungers for. Life is a world of swirling music. Your soul is in this world to dance and sing. Surrender your life as a wallflower. Join the rhythm, feel the beat, open to the melody. Cry. Feel something. Stay by the water. Let it teach you what it means to flow. Much of your pain and suffering is your soul saying *They are playing my favorite songs again. Can we please get up this time and lose ourselves in the ecstasy?*

LIFE IS NOT BEATING YOU UP. It is tenderizing you to be eaten alive by your Purpose. Breathe deeply, dear. Here comes your unbelievable dawn.

TO FIND YOURSELF, lose yourself over and over until you become an orphan to your identity. Then, wander the streets of your soul until you find something that feels like home.

A POET REMAINS in continuous divine orgasm at the wonder of this world. This is why poets need naps.

WHEN EARTH IS KISSED by rain, it blushes with infinite forms of life. What has died from the flood makes an offering of itself. So that new life may come.

After the rain, some things stink. They were decaying before the rain. The water touched their decay and brought out its stench. After the rains, other things release the sweetest aroma. Sweet things were happening within them, even before the water fell.

Things are lost in the floods. Things are gained. The deluge sweeps you into a closer encounter with suffering. Like babies at the first of life and those near to life's end, you taste the mystery and great expanse, and are flooded. You become the canyon, the arroyo gutted and resurfaced. Old, personal, private sedimentary layers are coughed up and visible to you and others. Detritus dances on your face. People get to see you without the makeup of daily routine and quasi stability. People get to see your morning (mourning) face.

When the rains come, how sad if you do not let yourself be flooded with suffering's divine thesis. Its teachings on how your way of life touches other souls and their living. Where the threads touch. The contagion of harm. Oppression's rancid breath. The violence of soulless individualism.

When the rains come, how sad if you do not let your heart dilate and rupture. If you do not collect epiphanies on sensitivity as you move through the aftermath. When mortality scrapes you to the bone, the truth of it should humble you. Forever. You ought never again hold yourself superior. When you look upon the stained life of others, you should see but diamonds in the dirt. Weep at that. Make the rains mean something. Fertility isn't promised. If you want a garden, you yourself must be willing to grow.

After the water, life grows silent in mourning, loud in conversation about what the rain meant and means. When it is dry and things are praying for water, habits and routines can seem eternal. The desert seems unchanging. But when rain comes and washes away your tightest attachments, your beliefs are shaken from the tree of your normalcy. Many of them drop to the ground and die. But in doing so, they make offerings for new life. If you mourn your beliefs and let them go, awakening comes. You gain brighter joys.

One moment, you believe you know yourself. In a flash, you are being tossed in a rampaging floodwater, all bearings lost. When you lose your old reference points, though it can be terrifying, it can grant you new eyes. Open them. Choose to see through them. See if you can see the great weaving that is this life.

DO YOU REMEMBER that one day when you were a child and you looked up at the sky and what you saw and felt exploded in your chest like a galaxy of awe? That feeling wasn't visiting you from another world. It lives in you. It is your energetic nature. Practice your awe. It will grow.

THAT THING YOU DID to harm yourself that you have felt shame for ever since. It is okay now. You can stop beating yourself for it. Compassion doesn't change what you did. It changes how what you did lives in you. You can be a kinder host to your past actions. To be well now, practice showing hospitality to your regrets. If they get good sleep in the bed of your more forgiving memory, they may feel Loved enough to vacate your premises entirely. You may even be moved to renovate your newly spacious soul.

GATHER MORE LOVE for you. You can find it in all the souls you water while you live in drought. Rain dance words.

YOU ARE NOT LIVING inside your life. You are living inside the story you tell yourself about your life. Make it a good story. Give it honey and flying wings. Soft landing places. Lofty heights to climb. Dispense with casting villains and heroes. Make everyone a suffering servant of the heart. Plant shade trees. And romance and intimacy and passion. Flood your story with purpose and wonder. And plenty of hope. Your ancestors would like to get a word in edgewise. Grant them the floor. I hope you let your story cry often and big. And that it is absolutely soaked and delirious with Love.

I WILL USE JUST A FEW words to say this. You are not a burial ground. Not a waste depot. You are a living garden. Things come and go from you. I am trying to say something about fear and its utensils of denial. You are sky. Not air in a bottle. Your suffering has so much space to roam and soothe itself. Be lifelike when you can.

YOUR PAIN HAS BEEN telling you stories again. Rumors and gossip and myth. Somewhere in there, it is telling you truth as well. Oh well. Your chore for the day is to separate the nightmare from the dream.

MAYBE GRIEF IN YOU is feeling claustrophobic. Maybe this is why it keeps pounding away at you from the inside. Maybe your grief needs more room to roam. For this, you have tears and laughter. Both yield many acres of space and flow. Maybe your grief just wants you to take it by the hand sometimes and walk it out in the fresh air or under the stars and let it say all the truest or most terrified things it wants to say.

IF YOUR PEOPLE picked cotton, corn, cane, cabbage, or cauliflower, they were doing sacred labor for their generations. You are their paycheck. Live your life in full bloom and with ancestral pride. Do not let your currency depreciate under the sweltering sun of a culture that devalues your people. Be the most beautiful, luscious, nourishing crop you can be.

SO MANY BEAUTIFUL ROSES growing in the soil of every living soul. From my first breath I have been breathless. This Creation is a miracle that keeps me weeping. Glory sings to me. The Grace in my heart sings back. The two Lovers meet in the middle of every moment and make a Love so divine, endless births come forth bringing more sacred music. How can you not dance ecstatic to this jubilation? How can you not give away your heart to this endless sun and infinite moon? Even writing these words I fall in Love again. Its boundless lake will not release me. And so I stay. For a lifetime I stay. If you want to find me, be willing to lose your clothes and leap into this water. I have heard the impossible music. It has taken me. I am not here. I am everywhere the holy song makes its reverent home.

HOW MANY OF THE SOULS throughout history whom you Love do you meet out on the dreamy vision-meadows or mountains where you send your soul wandering? If you are going to go to these places, you may as well be around those who move you while you are there. They are real and available to you even now. Just open your heart to them. They will appear.

THIS IS A STORY ABOUT ROSES. Of course, really it is a story about you. A person in pain could not bear the sight of the beauty of roses, which were growing everywhere in their country. So they cut down and uprooted roses wherever they could. The roses kept returning. The person lost so much blood to the rose thorns, they eventually died and were buried in an old, unkempt courtyard. Soon, the brightest colored roses grew from that very ground. Beauty is inescapable, dear one. You may as well join the festival.

BEWARE OF THOSE who ask you questions so they can place you in their social group cages. They don't want to know you. They want to cage you. Not every curiosity is motivated by Love. It can feel good to share of yourself. Take care to do so only with those who want you free.

YOU ARE SITTING on a mountain top, heaviness in your heart. A large black bird flies over the canopy far below you. Its lightness and freedom make you smile. You can feel its flight in your heart. You keep watching. The bird follows a stream as it continues drafting over the canopy. It is flying farther away from you, growing smaller in your vision. Still, you follow it, lightness gaining in your body. A part of you, maybe your soul itself, lifts up from rocky earth and takes flight. Now, elated, you are drafting and weightless. Your heart could burst. It does. You are air. Notice the birds of flight in your day, in your life. Be in awe. Join them.

GRIEF IS THE LOVE inside you shedding its skin, becoming a new form of Love. Grief is an ocean. Tidal and swelling. Untamed. You have yet to discover so much that lives in its depths. Your grief is so boundless and powerful, it scares you. You feel how easy it would be to drown in it. And yet, you can float its surface. It is saline. Buoyant. When you unclench your muscles and relax your body and breathing into grief's relentless ebbing, you can even experience a kind of clarified peace.

Just you, in your ocean. Everything on shore out of focus, appearing to be in slow motion. Just you, floating, in your ocean. You and everything it washes onto your emotional shore. You and everything it takes back into its belly. Unpredictable. Violent. Gentle. Clouded. Clear. Lapping against hard rocks, crashing onto sand. Becoming mist. Yes, becoming mist. Your grief. Eventually light enough to lift into sky.

I AM A PINECONE in a wildfire, dying to release the seeds of my soul. The inferno has annihilated my ego. Love's smoldering outburst is all that remains.

WANDERING THE DESERT, silence and solitude may gift you things you do not ask for. Such as your relative, coyote, his eyes speaking an ancient language. A tale of returning to the spirit world. Coyote is a desert trickster. What you see is not what you get. What you get is what you fail to see. Which is true for us now in the world. The Great Circle is turning, churning water like a wooden wheel. No one gets to say they are good anymore. Nothing matters but what we act against. Powered by what we act for. Who is lending a hand to the healing? Who is tearing down the barn where hell was wrought? These are the fires of reckoning now burning. May we see. So we may get free.

WHEN A PROFOUND knowing awakens in you, don't express it with lofty language as though you are on a cloud above the world. See if you can translate that flame into fruit and water. That way, all who hunger and thirst can feast with you.

IF YOU WANT TRUE PEACE, search your soul for the slave master in you and end its life. Only when we stop oppressing others with our convenience and comfort, with our unexamined way of life, do we begin to end the haunting of our spirit by life itself, a force that demands we answer to the demands of freedom.

ARRIVING TO ANOTHER PERSON'S SPACE and creative offering, then expressing critique, correction, or fault, is like sitting at someone's dinner table and criticizing the meal they have prepared and offered you. Either graciously accept the offering or quietly be on your way. Don't leave your ego or bitterness where someone has shared kindness. Don't defile someone's personal space, even if that space is public. Just because a meal doesn't suit you, doesn't mean it isn't someone else's dearly needed nutrition. Fathom grace.

WHEN THE CORN in the field is ready. And the sheep are nearly full coated. And the piñons drop. And the cool evening wind howls on the mesas. Your bones will birth the prophecy of your winter. A song your spirit will, at first, recite in whispers. Your minerals will surge inside you, helplessly in Love with being. A delirious tidal ache.

You will go naked and swim out into the black blessing of a bottomless bay. Still protected by layers of denial, you will search for the sun of truth even as you fear it. Something old, like the memory of memory, will come over you. You will lose your tolerance for veils.

As you at last let truth's sun scorch you, others will back away, aversive to your new passion of divine, solar intimacy. But they will be starving for the same intimacy. Dying. So you will feed them their own glory. For they have forgotten, it is they who both prayed for and gestate all the things born of sun.

IF YOU ARE FEELING OVERWHELMED, maybe you are under-welcomed. Maybe you have not welcomed yourself all the way inside your soul. The heart of your soul is a place of tranquility and grace. There, you can remain at ease even when the world's tides crash all around you. Welcome yourself inside the heart of your soul. Rooms exist there that you have not experienced. Treasure chests are still unopened. No need to be an anxious child afraid the ice cream will run out. There is always more peace for you, dear soul. Your spiritual practices do not promise you peace. But they do *peace-ify* your practices. Which is a mercy when you need to feel safe inside.

SOME DAYS YOU EAT TOFU and listen to harp music. Other days you grub grits and bang blues rap. Your movement between these is beautiful. Your self-permission to move is the birth spark of freedom.

MAYBE THE EXHAUSTED FLOWER that is your soul only wants the lush pillow of you at peace.

I DO NOT KNOW how you take your coffee or tea, though I hope you will let me pour this Love for you. You can survive for a lifetime being deficient in some nutrients. Not for long can you survive a Love deficiency. Today, I watched a flock of pelicans skirt inches over the ocean face. They seemed to fly unnaturally slow. As though in prayer. Now I see the connection, dear one. You are at your best in a prayerful condition, your soul open and oriented to Sacredness.

If you grow still enough inside, you begin to hear the holy praise you have always yearned for. Divine beauty is in you, all around you, and of you. Dilate to it. Let it impregnate you out of this life of empty imitation. You do not have to stand at the well imagining its cold water on your lips. The day is hot and you are thirsty. Bring up the overflowing bucket. Drink.

WILL YOU COME SIT with me under this almond tree? Here, next to me. Thank you. Now... I am not going to speak. I am going to listen. Here is what your soul is saying to me:

When I was young, I felt too little, the world too big. Now I feel too old, the world too young and overwhelming. I used to chase butterflies and fireflies, laughing. Now monsters chase me in my dreams. They are not laughing.

I used to cry as freely as a spring sky. Now I have so many tears, but I prohibit myself from crying them free. They burrow into me farther than I can see. I used to feel full of life and empty of expectation. Now I just feel empty, except for the weight of endless expectation. Honestly, I just want to be held. Will you hold me?

I will, dear soul. I will. For I believe you are only part of the way across a surreal meadow, feeling like you are at its end. I will hold you because your tenderness is a voice saying *I feel like I can cross this meadow. I just need some safe affection and to be sincerely affirmed, please.* So I will hold you. I only ask that you hold me, too. Thank you for joining me under this almond tree.

MAYBE YOU DO NOT HAVE TO solve your life today. Maybe your sincere desire to heal and grow is sufficient labor for the moment. Breathe faith in your soul yearnings. They work on your behalf even while you sleep. Yes, you can rest and still grow your life. In fact, rest is the romance your life may desire most. It wants the intimacy of you nurturing you. Watch what it does with those heavenly kisses.

WHEN YOU WAKE AFTER swimming in the spirit world ocean all night, some things want to come with you into the mundane dimension of your day. Insights, memories, epiphanies, revelations, glories. These are the seeings that human daytimes burn off like morning dew.

Have ceremonies that invite these visitors to remain close to you. Stay open and connected. Like when you were a baby. Be in the other world, dipped in the divine and free of ego and identity and group attachments.

You are an artery carrying oxygenated blood from that mystic world into the depleted body of this world. Stay open and aerobic. Dilated and enlightened. Bring the blood. Live today as a mystic. Retire from your earthly occupations and be a living window. We have lost our sight and cannot see the miracle for what it is. Harvest what sleep does to your soul. Delight the human market with your farm to table ministry.

HAVE YOU EVER MADE LOVE that feels so good your entire body feels like it is on the verge of evaporating into molecules of bliss? Your life can be like this. In both cases, sexual and mundane, the key is not your desire. It is your surrender. Not into pleasure, but out of fear-soaked control and clenching.

This life wants to sacredly touch all your favorite places and to be sacredly touched by you in all its favorite places. It wants an intimacy of trust and honesty. It wants you to stop pretending and performing, to be present and unadorned and real. No games or misdirection. No manipulation or angling. Just sheer humility so complete it shatters your composure and leaves you a willowy, supple vessel for the ecstatic passion of divine Love.

IF YOU SAY YOU DO NOT LIKE POETRY, it is likely that the poetry you were force-fed in school and childhood was culturally dead to your life. And that the force-feeding itself was lifeless. If this is so, maybe it is your idea of poetry that you do not like.

We know your secrets. The way you enjoy the crunch of cucumber in your mouth. How summer's peak vibration leaves you both seduced and unfulfilled. Your blushing at the sexuality of moon's monthly pregnancy. So much other private savoring and succumbing. Water's magic.

Night's mystery. The rebellion of tears. Cruelty. Kindness. Glances. Romances between seasonings in your food. Loneliness. Hopeful pessimism. Pessimistic hopefulness. Dreams you drag into day. Your body's functioning is poetry. The way it heals is a poetic masterpiece. Your emotions are lyrics. Everything you are is poetry. Even the way your ancestors still recite their favorite lines through your organic ways of being you.

THIS THOUGHT WON'T TAKE LONG. I am hungry and you are, too. There are words for what your pain and joy do together inside your soul, though humans have forgotten the sacred language. Let's try this: Life itself is busy cooking in the kitchen of your soul. It uses all your spices. All your wild herbs. And every meal it serves sings these flavorful lyrics: *I am so in Love with you.*

I LOOKED FOR YOU in palaces of power. They said you were roaming the hills. I looked for you there. They said you were last seen naked in the sea talking with the night sky. I looked for you there. They said you had just left and were rolling down the winery hills, laughing. I looked for you there. They said I had just missed you. That you had joined a caravan of seekers and zealots. I looked for you there.

I looked for you by cold dawn streams. On the broiling gypsum of deserts. In the moans of Lovers and tears of sufferers become healers. In the middle of children screaming delight. On the far side of moon. In attics with old books to the ceilings. In fireplaces barren of ash. In sacred spaces where women had just given birth. In saunas where doulas exhale. In fox dens. High in canopies. Under willows. Over canyons. In temples. At the edge of fear. In patches of gloom. In threads of breeze. Outside taverns. In gutters. Down the street from praise. In the wet eyes of elders. In the June of youth.

I looked for you in prayers. Prophets. Pride. I looked for you in memories. I looked for you everywhere. At last, I found you where I was not looking. You were nowhere. Which is why you are everywhere.

OUR SOULS ARE SO WOVEN, dear one. I feel so close to you. We are swimming together in the same impossible lake. All the stars are watching us. Moon is blushing. Sky is chiding the frisky comets. When you dive down into water depths, I follow. When I surface, there you are, a smile on your glistening face. I start to tell you stories. You finish them. You drop tears. My hands were already at your cheek to catch your grace.

We say so much in this silence. So much silence in what we say. All we hear now is water splashing its song of joy. You and I break so many rules. Unravel so many mysteries that we kiss on their lips before we ravel them up again. Morning and night chaperone us. It does not matter. We know how to communion alone or in the brilliance of universes.

GOD MAKES LOVE WITH ME and words come through that you call poetry. My molecules and cells flood with Grace and Glory. I have nowhere to put this divine abundance. I pour it out to you. To you. Humans stumble between destroying and creating this world. The offspring of both impulses are a wildfire my heart cannot hold. I apologize for all this gushing. No. I do not.

Someone built a dam to contain my soul water. The water laughed and demolished the dam. If anyone is living downstream in tents of fear, they had better evacuate. I cannot hold back this purging. Roses dream and I feel it all. I live by weeping. My heart is a delicate tremble. You walk out at night, your bare feet on the wet grass, and stare at the sky, wondering. All your wondering is in me. Night walks out on the wet grass of my soul and wonders me.

LOOK HOW RAIN JOINS WITH SOIL to turn what was hard into a suppleness for transformation and birth. You and I, we live so much of our lives as hard dirt clumps. Sometimes, breaking down is how we let our souls flood with rain-blessed earth, which is God, which is our medicine. Are you grieving, dear one? I know the ache spreads through you like a harsh, insensitive wind. You feel so alone. I hope you can remember now, Love lives too in small and intangible things. In the air you breathe.

You are seaside on a blanket in sun and breeze. The spirit of those you Love is the ocean mist on your skin. So much Love is with you now. I hope you will let yourself break down. What comes from that is your most beautiful art.

INSIDE LOVE'S SANCTUARY, we cannot ask for too much. There is no asking. Only the Holy response.

WHILE YOU AND I ARE IN THIS WORLD, we have been given the gift of being able to paint the most beautiful mural of Love in every barrio and pueblo. Will you. Join me?

I WAKE UP WEEPING every current of Love's infinite river. Including pain. I live the nubile day weeping. I fall asleep weeping. What an immeasurable gift. To be so fluent in the fluidity of Grace.

PRECIOUS SOUL. May I please share something with you? Your grief is not an inconvenience. I pray that when you are hurting and lonely, you will ask someone safe, the right someone, to hold you. Whether they are near or far, please ask them to hold you, in spirit or form. Allow them that blessing. Let them fulfill their Love. Your pain is not a burden. It is an honest mercy. Ask to be held sacredly. Be that brave. Sometimes, Love needs an invitation to offer its affection gift.

YOUR PAIN URGES YOU to find a million reasons why a healing practice will not work for you. You resent even the offering of hopeful ideas. Please feel no shame in this. Even the shade seeks shade, where some things do grow. If you want life's entire bounty though, hold your pessimism and negativity when they arise. Sing to them, then set them free. Love yourself enough to dare something fertile. You say *I've tried that. It doesn't work*. Healing is not something you try. It is a lifelong devotion. Dare that ocean.

Two crows fly, one after the other. You ask *What determines which one leads*? It depends what they are flying toward. If it is fear, the one most seduced by fear takes the lead. If Love is their destination, you know the Lover leads the way.

IF YOU MADE IT THIS FAR, you must be carrying medicine enough for everyone. Go get us some drinking cups. Any kind will do. I've brought Glory wine for this occasion. I hope you took a nap today. We are going to be at this until dawn.

If this book touched you, you can touch it back.

Please kindly consider writing an **online reader review** at various booksellers. Reviews are a valuable way to support the life of a book and especially an independent author.

Freely **post social media photos** of you or others with the book, just the book itself, or passages from the book. Please kindly include the hashtag **#jaiyajohn.**

I deeply cherish your support of my books and our Soul Water Rising rehumanizing mission around the world.

BOOK ANGEL PROJECT

Your book purchases support our global *Book Angel Project,* which provides grants, scholarships, and book donations for vulnerable youth, and places gift copies of my *medicine books* throughout communities worldwide, to be discovered by the souls who need them. These books are left where hearts are tender: hospitals, nursing homes, prisons, wellness centers, group homes, mental health clinics, and other community spaces.

If you are fortunate to discover one of our *Book Angel* gift books, please kindly post a photo of you with the book on Instagram, using the hashtag **#jaiyajohn,** or email us at **books@soulwater.org.** Thank you much!

I Will Read for You:
The Voice and Writings of Jaiya John

A podcast. Voice medicine to soothe your soul, from poet, author, and spoken word artist Jaiya John. Bedtime bliss. Morning meditation. Daytime peace. Comfort. Calm. Soul food. Come, gather around the fire. Let me read for you. **Spotify. Apple. Wherever podcasts roam.**

Dr. Jaiya John was orphan-born on Ancient Puebloan lands in the high desert of New Mexico, and is an internationally recognized freedom worker, author, and poet. Jaiya is the founder of Soul Water Rising, a global *rehumanizing* mission to eradicate oppression that has donated thousands of Jaiya's books in support of social healing, and offers grants and scholarships to displaced and vulnerable youth. He is the author of numerous books, including *Fragrance After Rain, Daughter Drink This Water,* and, *Freedom: Medicine Words for your Brave Revolution.* Jaiya writes, narrates, and produces the podcast, *I Will Read for You: The Voice and Writings of Jaiya John,* and is the founder of *Freedom Project,* a global initiative reviving traditional, ancestral gathering and storytelling practices to fertilize social healing and liberation. He is a former professor of social psychology at Howard University, and has spoken to over a million people worldwide and audiences as large as several thousand. Jaiya is a former National Science Foundation fellow, and holds doctorate and master's degrees in social psychology from the University of California, Santa Cruz, with a focus on intergroup and race relations. As an undergraduate, he attended Lewis & Clark College in Portland, Oregon, and lived in Kathmandu, Nepal, where he studied Tibetan Holistic Medicine through independent research with Tibetan doctors and trekked to the base camp of Mt. Everest. His Indigenous soul dreams of frybread, sweetgrass, bamboo in the breeze, and turtle lakes whose poetry is peace.

Learn more at: JAIYAJOHN.COM

Jacqueline V. Carter and Kent W. Mortensen served graciously, faithfully, and skillfully as editors for *Fragrance After Rain*. I am forever grateful for their Love labor.

Secure a Jaiya John keynote, talk, or reading:

jaiyajohn.com

OTHER BOOKS BY JAIYA JOHN

Jaiya John titles are available online where books are sold. To learn more about this and other books by Jaiya, to order discounted bulk quantities, or to learn about Soul Water Rising's global freedom work, please visit us at:

jaiyajohn.com

books@soulwater.org

@jaiyajohn (IG FB TW YT)

CPSIA information can be obtained
at www.ICGtesting.com
Printed in the USA
BVHW072028011221
622869BV00010B/368

9 780998 780269